To Pak Ou cave temples 30 km by boat about 2 hours
To B. P
B. Phonsaat
B. Mai
Luang Prabang Airport
Nam Khan River
Phetsarat Rd.
B. Phanom-Noy
B. Phanom
Nam Khan River
B. Houadon
29
Temple (Wat)
Historic Building
Market (Talat)
Museum
N
Houaymao

Ancient Luang Prabang & Laos

To Monica

best wishes

Denise Heywood

15-10-15

RIVER
BOOKS

ANCIENT
LUANG PRABANG
& LAOS
DENISE HEYWOOD

First published and distributed in 2006 by River Books
Reprinted 2008

This revised and updated edition 2014

River Books
396 Maharaj Road, Tatien, Bangkok 10200
Tel. 66 2 222-1290, 225-0139, 224-6686
Fax. 66 2 225-3861
E-mail: order@riverbooksbk.com
www.riverbooksbk.com

ISBN 978-616-7339-45-0

Editors: Narisa Chakrabongse and Chris Shelley
Production supervision: Paisarn Piammattawat
Design: Narisa Chakrabongse, Suparat Sudcharoen and Ruetairat Nanta

Title page: *Aerial view showing the meeting point of the Mekong and Nam Khan rivers.*
© Thierry Renavand, *Luang Phabang: an architectural journey.*

Print and bound in Thailand by Sirivatana Interprint Public Co., Ltd.

ACKNOWLEDGEMENTS

We would like to thank the American Embassy in Vientiane, Laos for their generous financial help with this new edition.

Grateful thanks for their help go to:

Francis Engelmann of UNESCO and the Heritage House.

Madame Vayakone Bodhisane, Managing Director of Diethelm Travel, Vientiane.

The Grand Hotel, Luang Prabang.

University of Northern Illinois for many of the historic old pictures of Luang Prabang from Treasures of Luang Prabang published in 2000 by The Ministry of Foreign Affairs of Lao P.D.R.

PHOTO CREDITS:

All photos Denise Heywood except where indicated otherwise.

Additional photos:
École Française d'Extrême-Orient
National Museum of Luang Prabang
Louis Delaporte
Mission Pavie
S Bounthieng
Pha Khamfa
Prida
Vieng Xay Soudarot
Paisarn Piammattawat (PP)
Oraphan Chaivorarat (OC)

CONTENTS

Introduction

"On 25 July, 1861, I reached Luang Prabang, a delightful little town, set in its amphitheatre of mountains … a paradise."
Henri Mouhot

High up in the mist-shrouded mountains of northern Laos, on a promontory of the broad Mekong river, is Luang Prabang, a town of glittering Buddhist temples and barefoot monks. For centuries, it was a remote place with a dream-like quality, as if time here had stood still. With the centre of the town dominated by Mount Phousi, the 'marvellous mountain', with a golden temple perched on the top, its beauty is twofold, a combination of a dramatic natural setting and a rich legacy of sacred art and architecture.

Between the 16th and 19th centuries, when Luang Prabang was a royal capital and religious centre, more than 60 wooden monasteries and shrines were built, sumptuously gilded, stuccoed and stencilled, and set in tranquil courtyards with chapels and pagodas. The surrounding verdant mountains enhanced the jewel-like identity of Luang Prabang, making it seems like a hidden treasure and imbuing it with an other-worldly atmosphere.

Its remoteness was due in part to Laos being a landlocked country, with the Mekong river as its sole lifeline. As a result, it had limited contact with the outside world. The ancient kingdom of Luang Prabang, called *Lane Xang,* had political relations with nearby Lan Na, in present day Thailand, and Sipsong Pan Na, to the north, in China. Caravans of traders, travelling by boat or by elephant, journeyed down from Southern China, Tibet, Tonkin

Opposite: *The Mekong River, the main artery of Laos.*

Below: *An old picture of Wat Xieng Thong.*

View of the Mekong.

Below: *An etching of Luang Prabang viewed from the other side of the Mekong. Note That Chomsi on top of the mountain.*

Opposite: *Wat Mai's dazzling verandah.*

and Burma. In 1828 Laos became a tributary to Siam and remained so until the arrival of French colonisers who annexed it in 1893 when it became part of the Indochinese Union.

With the arrival of the French in the 19th century came a new wave of building. Elegant colonial villas were constructed in Luang Prabang, blending harmoniously with the temples and secular architecture. These villas were perfectly adapted to the tropical environment, surrounded by lush greenery, palm trees and exuberantly coloured bougainvillea. The French embellished Luang Prabang, but changed it, giving it a dual identity, Eastern and Western. The fusion of these two disparate cultures resulted in a singular beauty.

In 1995 Luang Prabang was nominated as a UNESCO World Heritage Site to protect its fragile culture, a status which extends to 177 sacred structures which make up the 34 temples that have survived, together with 443 civic buildings. It also encompasses 183 ponds, together with their fish and vegetation, maintained in their natural state. Luang Prabang's remarkably well preserved townscape illustrates a key stage in the blending of these two distinct cultural traditions and is considered to be the best preserved town in Southeast Asia.

Populated by monks – although increasingly by tourists – the town resonates with a spiritual aura. Yet, in spite of the growth of tourism, it still has an atmosphere of seclusion, a place apart from the modern world. In an age where change is so swift and momentous, this sense of isolation is an intrinsic part of the beauty of Luang Prabang and gives it a unique identity.

Lin-Ngan
Sin Tschou Fu
Nan Ning Fu
KUANG-TU
Sib Song Panna
TONG-KING
Muong
Bak Ninh
Hai Dzuong
HANOI
Ba Wi
Hung Hoa
Son La
Dien Bien P.
I. Tsieng Mui Tao
I. Ke-Bao
I. Wai Tschou
I. Kao Ba
Do Son
Nam Dinh
Ninh Binh
I. Basch Long Wi
MB. VON TONG-KING
LUANG-PRABANG
Pu Ho
Luang Prabang
Mekong
Pu Lor
Tran Ninh
Thanh Hoa
I. Bien Son
Vinh (Ting Nghe)
HAI
Wu Schi
K. Bastion
ESISCHE
STAATEN
Lachon
M. Pre
Nong-Chai
Pu-Thai
M. Lachon
K. Bung-Kiua
Kwang-Binh (Dong Hoi)
Tiger-I.
K. Lai
Rhhang
Hué
Thuan-An
Turan
B. v. Turan
I. Kulao-Scham
K. Kaholai
SIAM
Nachon-Sawan
Korat
Nam Mun
Bassak
Boloven
Lagrée-Sp.
Moi
Sedang
K. Bantam
Kulao-Rai
K. Batangan
B. Prabat
AJUTHIA
Phom Dong Rek
Dong Paja Pai
BANGKOK
Meklong
Petschaburi
Petriu
Aranh
Sisophon
Angkor
Battambang
Tonle Sap
Bahnar
Rade
N. Bason
N. Tam Phong Doa
KAMBODJA
Stieng
Kratie
Sambor
K. Liant
I. Samit
Koh Sabap
Pran
I. Tschang
Prabat-Ceb
B. Pursat
Kampong Cham
Pnom-Penh
I. Kut
I. Kong
Kampot
I. Rong
B. v. Kampong Som
I. Tron
(Phu Kwok)
SAIGUN
K. Kega
I. Vache
I. Cecir de Ter
K. Padara
KOCHINCHINA
K. S. Jacques
Halbinsel
von Kamau
MB. VON
SIAM
Tau
Saui-B
I. Pennan
I. Samui
Pulo Uai
Pulo Dama
Pulo Pandjang
Pulo Kondor
K. Kambodja

Land and People

"When the water level falls, the ants eat the fish; when the water level rises, the fish eat the ants." Lao saying

Land

Laos is a small, landlocked country of steep mountains and impenetrable forests, cut through by the Mekong river. Bordered by Burma, Thailand, Vietnam and China, the area remained remote and uncharted until the 19th century and was unknown in the West.

Covering an area of 236,800 square kilometres, Laos is two-thirds rugged mountainous terrain, part of the Annamite range of mountains, reaching a maximum elevation of 2,820 metres. With limestone peaks and hills swathed in dense primary forest, it has a pristine ecology. Lush vegetation of dipterocarps, which grow to 30 metres in height, make up the top layers of deciduous monsoon forest. There is a middle canopy where teak, *Tectona grandis,* rosewood and other hardwoods grow, together with smaller trees, grasses, mosses, fern and bamboo, *Bambusa,* so hardy and versatile that it is used in house construction, for scaffolding and even as irrigation pipes. Coconut palms, *Cocos nucifera,* abound, as do banana trees and fruit trees, ranging from mango, *Mangifera indica,* to papaya, *Carica papaya.* Mulberry trees, *Morus,* are cultivated to feed silkworms. The white Mulberry, *Morus alba,* is used, as well as *Morus multicaulis,* which produces succulent leaves for the silkworms. Timber is a source of revenue but conservationists have tried to curb logging and deforestation by setting up National Biodiversity Conservation Areas.

The Mekong river forms a natural border with Thailand and flows for 1,900 kilometres in Laos, a third of its length which is calculated at between 4,350-4,909 kilometres, after rising in China from a 5,000 metre elevation on the Tibetan Plateau. Broad and shallow, its tributaries are navigable only in the rainy season. At its widest point in southern Laos, at Si Phan Don, it measures 14 kilometres, creating an area of thousands of small islands. As well as being a source of fish, the principal source of protein for the Lao people, the Mekong deposits fertile alluvial silt in the soils around its flood plains, and has always been the main artery of travel and trade. Marco Polo was probably the first European to cross the Mekong in the 13th century. His notes were used by all subsequent travellers, including Gerrit van Wuysthoff in the 17th century and Francis Garnier, who first mapped the river, in 1868.

The Mekong Secretariat was formed in 1957 to harness the waters that flow from China through Laos, Cambodia and Vietnam, for irrigation and hydro-power. Although plans to dam the Mekong remain controversial, the Nam Ngum river, close to Vientiane, has been dammed to form a reservoir that provides hydro-electric power which is sold to Thailand. But plans to proceed with a 'mega' hydropower dam on the Mekong at

A river in Northern Laos.

Opposite: *Indo-China coloured lithograph by Standford's Geog. London 1904.*

Looking across the Mekong from Luang Prabang.

Boats to Pak Ou on the Mekong.

A girl with a parrot.

Ice Cream Seller Mr Leng.

Marigolds.

Xayaburi, in northern Laos, to be completed in 2020, remain controversial, as do 11 other dam projects for the lower Mekong river running through Southeast Asia, including the Nam Theun II which began operation in 2010. Of concern in Luang Prabang are projects using explosives to smash rocky reefs on the Mekong to allow ships to navigate between Southern China and Luang Prabang. This is also destroying fish stocks. The prized Mekong Giant catfish, *pla buk,* is fished in June, July and August on its upward journey in the Mekong, but its numbers are declining. At the lower reaches of the Mekong are Irrawaddy dolphins, an endangered species of which only a few remain.

Wildlife includes the leopard, Javan mongoose, goat-antelopes, gibbons, langurs, Malayan sunbear, Asiatic black bear and pangolins. Many of these are endangered species and rarely seen. The 19th century explorer Henri Mouhot found a variety of insects and animals, including a scarabeus beetle, named after him, *Mouhotia gloriosa.* There are many varieties of birds and butterflies, as well as dragonflies, grasshoppers, crickets and cicadas, the latter with their inimitable sounds at dawn and dusk. Sadly, much wildlife disappeared during the war years as it was hunted for food, a practice that continues today. However, research in the forests has started again and scientists are now discovering new species of animals, such as rabbits and deer.

The many ponds in Luang Prabang, so essential to the ecology, abound in lotus, *Nelumba nucifera,* in varying shades of pink or red, and water hyacinth, *Eichornia crassipes.* This latter plant was introduced from abroad and has proliferated out of control. The large leaves of the lotus, beloved of frogs and dragonflies, lie flat on the surface of the water.

In some temple compounds there are majestic old banyan trees, with branches that send out shoots which grow down to the soil and root to form secondary trunks, and pipal trees, *Ficus religiosa,* giving shade and venerated as the tree under which the Buddha received enlightenment. Within the *wats* is also an array of brilliantly coloured flowers from bougainvillea, a dense bush of brilliant pink, crimson, purple or orange flowers, to fragrant frangipani, *Plumeria acutifolia,* known in Laos as *Doc champa,* the national flower. The heady perfume of this white and yellow or pink and yellow flower, which symbolises joy in life, is distinctive and the petals are used in traditional dance performances. *Plumeria* reach a height of 10 to 20 metres, their widely spaced succulent branches are round or pointed, and long waxy leaves cluster near the branch tips. Flowering lasts about three months at a time, producing new blooms every day. When picked, a bloom kept in water will last for several days. Around temples the fallen flowers, scattered on the ground, add a romantic atmosphere and continue to emanate their fragrance. Hibiscus, the trumpet shaped orange, red or yellow flower, also abounds, as do velvety white orchids, often hanging in individual baskets on verandahs.

The betelnut, product of the areca palm tree, *Areca catechu,* is widely used in Laos. Made up of the nut, with lime, and wrapped in betel vine, *Piper betel,* this is used as a mild stimulant by keeping it in the mouth where it stains the gums and teeth red.

Betel was used during social functions, and this habit, practised for centuries, gave rise to the creation of ornate little silver boxes in which to keep the betelnuts. Its use continues to prevail in the countryside, but less so in the cities where its associated practice of spitting is viewed as distasteful.

Laos also grows the opium poppy, *Papaver somniferum,* traditionally a cash crop of the Yao and Hmong people, in the northern part of the country which forms the notorious 'golden triangle' with Thailand and Burma. It came from Southern China in the 19th century and was once an important commodity. Between 1839-1842 and 1856-60, opium wars were fought between China and Britain. Although it is now illegal, its growth flourished during the Vietnam War. Other crops, including coffee, tea and maize, have been encouraged to replace poppies.

Laos has a tropical, monsoon climate. The word 'monsoon' is from Arabic, *mawsim,* meaning season, and refers to the winds. The rainy season starts in May as the southwest monsoon brings rain clouds across from the Indian Ocean, and lasts until October. Luang Prabang receives about 1,360 millimetres of rain per annum. The dry season starts in October as the northeast monsoon blows from central Asia until March, heralding a dry and cooler period. In between March and May is the hot season. Temperatures range between 10 and 35 degrees celsius, with the cooler weather prevailing in the northern mountains. The advance and retreat of the monsoon rains govern the cycle of wet rice cultivation, rice being the staple diet of the Laotians.

In Luang Prabang, the confluence of the Mekong and the Nam Khan rivers result in flat lands that produce abundant rice crops, especially on the banks of the river which are enriched by the river's nutrients as the waters recede in the dry season. Rice, the staple diet of Laotians, is the seed of the monocot plant Oryza sativa. Farmers plant rice seed in a protected bed and as seedlings mature transplant them into fields that have been prepared by flooding and ploughing, by water-buffalo. When the rice plant

Lotus.

Bougainvillea.

Frangipani.

Vegetables growing by the river.

An Ahka hill tribe girl. Different tribes have distinctive clothing and head dresses.

Hill tribe woman.

Hmong girl in her traditional costume.

turns from green to yellow it is ready for harvesting, often done by women, using a sickle to cut the stalks. The grain is separated from the chaff by threshing. The spirit, *phi,* of the rice is honoured with offerings before cultivation, and the image of the Buddha in the position 'calling for rain' is highly symbolic for Laos, as the rice crop depends on rain. Festivals mark the end of the dry season and the end of the rainy season heralds more festivities in the form of boat races.

The country is divided into 17 provinces, *khoueng,* including that of Luang Prabang. These in turn are subdivided into districts, *muang,* and villages, *ban.*

People

Archaeological evidence suggests that the Lao people originally migrated south from China, being proto-Indo-Chinese or Mon-Khmer, and were influenced by the ideas and cultures of India, via Burma, Thailand and Cambodia. They mingled with Ai Lao or Lao Tai, indigenous hill tribes, and formed multi-ethnic communities, *muang,* principalities, evolving into small, feudal kingdoms whose rulers' power extended out across the valleys and mountains. Eventually they united under Lane Xang, the Kingdom of Laos.

Laos is less a nation state and more a collection of different tribes and languages. Ethnically diverse, Laos's population of five million people is made up of four major ethnolinguistic families, according to UNESCO, which consist of Lao Tai, Mon Khmer, Hmong, Yao and Tibeto-Burman. Within these are 47 official ethnolinguistic groups, including Lao, Lao Loum, Lao Tai, Lao Theung, Lao Soung, Yao, Hmong, Akha and Ho. The country's cultural wealth is due in part to this diversity, with a mixture of languages, aesthetic traditions and religious beliefs.

Among the many ethnic minorities, the Hmong are the best known and can often be seen in Luang Prabang. Hmong, meaning 'mankind', are animists who were forced south from China into Laos by opium farmers. Renowned for growing opium poppies, although outlawed by the government, they live at high altitudes and practise shifting cultivation, moving villages when surrounding land is exhausted. They are renowned for their independence and pride and because of their warrior qualities, were recruited by America's Central Intelligence Agency (CIA) during the Vietnam War. The extended families live in long-houses on the ground rather than on stilts, and the women are skilled weavers. They wear distinctive embroidered clothes embellished with ornate silver neck rings and heavy silver chokers and earrings. Nowadays they come to Luang Prabang to sell their handicrafts in the recently established Hmong market, which caters to tourists. But in their villages they preserve their old way of life, with village story tellers maintaining the oral tradition.

With a comparatively small population and the survival of oral traditions, families and groups remained connected to one another without the need for family names. Until 1943, there were no surnames in Laos, only first names. In René de Berval's book, *Kingdom of Laos,* Thao Nhouy Abhay, one of the contributors, writes that no child had ever been given the same name as his father until the Governor General of Indo-China instituted a decree on 28 July 1943 that each person should have a family name in addition to a personal name. There were already titles for social rank in existence, which included *Chao,* for princes and noblemen, *Thao* for mandarins or sons of mandarins, and *Agna* or *Nang* for princesses who were the wives or daughters of mandarins.

Thao Nhouy Abhay laments the disappearance of many of these titles but writes of the "extreme courtesy" of the Laotians that has led to many people taking the title *Agna,* "a custom to which one cannot take exception." He also refers to the "astonishing crop of surnames", many of Pali or Sanskrit origins, that arose in the wake of the decree, creating a plethora of *Khams, Phengs* and *Phanhs*.

Rice wine production in Ban Zang Hai, 25 kilometres north of Luang Prabang on the way to the Pak Ou caves. (PP)

Language

The official language is Lao, *Phaasa Lao,* a tonal language of the Tai family. *Abugida* is the writing system, similar to that of Thailand. The Lao alphabet has 33 consonants and 28 vowels. There are five main dialects, and each is divided into sub-dialects.

Older people still speak French. Young people are eager to learn English.

Common Courtesies

The generally accepted form of greeting is the *nop.* The palms of the hands are placed together in a position of prayer, at chest level, but not touching the body. The higher the hands, the greater the sign of respect. The *nop* is accompanied by a slight bow of respect.

When entering a *wat* or a home, people remove their shoes.

The head is considered the most sacred part of the body, and the feet the least holy part. One never points one's feet at other people nor in the direction of the Buddha in a *wat.*

Harvesting rice, the staple diet in Laos.

A Brief History

"Gigantic peaks they had to scale whose heights are known to none, Conquer they must. And the prince, victorious, reached the highest summit." Lao song

Luang Prabang market when Auguste Pavie visited.
(Courtesy University of Illinois)

Early Lao history is little documented. But archaeological and historical evidence suggests that the early indigenous population of this mountainous, landlocked region, the *Lao Theung,* one of the many ethnic Tai people, probably originated in China and migrated south, mingling with the *Lao Loum.* There were early feudal kingdoms, including Muang Swa, the earlier name of the area of Luang Prabang, and smaller kingdoms in the north such as Muang Sing, which were brought under one ruler in Luang Prabang only after the 14th century.

Luang Prabang became the royal capital in 1353 when Fa Ngum, a great warrior, became the first king of *Lane Xang Hom Khao,* the Land of a Million Elephants and the White Parasol. At that time there were many elephants in Luang Prabang, and they became the symbol of the Kingdom, although today they survive only in the forests. But elephants were also symbolic of warfare, as Martin Stuart-Fox points out in *A History of Laos.* Warfare was endemic in mainland Southeast Asia, he writes, fought by large conscripted armies of foot soldiers and elephant corps. "The very name *Lane Xang*, A Million Elephants, stated a claim to military power."

Lao history is interwoven with legends, and in mythological accounts Fa Ngum was said to have descended from the god of the sky, Khun Borom, and was thus revered as having divine status. Fa Ngum, son of a Tai prince, was raised at the court of Angkor in Cambodia and married a Khmer princess, Keo Kaengkanya. He received the Pra Bang Buddha, a golden Buddha statue said to have been cast in Ceylon, but fashioned in the style of 13th century Khmer sculpture, as a gift from his father-in-law, the King of Angkor, Phaya Sirichanta. This Buddha statue was to become the royal palladium and protector of the Lao kingdom. When Keo Kaengkanya died in 1368, Fa Ngum is rumoured to have become so dissolute that he was deposed and his son, Sam Saentai, became king in 1373.

Laos, surrounded by powerful neighbours, was constantly invaded by the Chinese, Vietnamese, Siamese and Khmers. The Khmer empire expanded into Laos between the 9th-15th centuries, introducing new ideas and leaving a legacy of archaeological remains in the south, notably Wat Phu. The Kingdom of Luang Prabang continued to maintain political relations with Lan Na and Chiang Mai in Thailand, and Sipsong Pan Na in China.

King Sam Saentai (Lord of Three Hundred Thousand Tais) ruled until 1416. During a reign that lasted 43 years, he built up an administrative structure as well as military strength. Trade increased and the kingdom prospered. The study of Buddhism,

Opposite: *Elephant procession on Pi Mai, Laos New Year of 1932.* (Courtesy University of Illinois Treasures of Luang Prabang)

Vigil around the Pra Bang Buddha image. Note the hanglin, *the long wooden pole in the form of a* naga *used for aspersing the holy image with water.*
(Courtesy University of Illinois)

a religion that had come peacefully with trade from India, was encouraged and temples were built. He was followed by King Lan Kham Deng, 1416-27, before a succession of short-lived rulers that culminated in the the reign of King Photthisarat, 1520-47. Under his reign Vientiane, known in Lao as Vieng Chan, City of the Moon, became an important centre of trade and religion. In 1527, this deeply religious king outlawed animist sacrifices to the spirits and ordered the destruction of Luang Prabang's most revered shrine. Wat Aham was later built on this ancient site. 1527 also saw the building of Wat Sangkhalok on what was said to be the oldest Buddhist site in Luang Prabang, on a tributary of the Mekong, called Nam Dong. Photthisarat married a Lan Na princess, Yotkamtip, and in 1545, his son, Setthathirat, claimed the Lan Na throne. Setthathirat, whose statue takes pride of place in front of Wat That Luang in Vientiane, ruled from 1548-1571 and was the last great king of Lane Xang. After his father's death, Setthathirat returned from Lan Na to Lane Xang with the Pra Kaeo, the Emerald Buddha, another renowned image. Both the Pra Bang and the Pra Kaeo Buddhas images were particularly sacred and believed to be inhabited by spirits. Their proximity to each other could be disastrous, it was believed.

Setthathirat organised a strategic alliance with the Siamese kingdom of Ayutthaya in 1560, and started the construction of Wat Xieng Thong in Luang Prabang. But he then decided to move his capital to Vientiane in 1563 as Luang Prabang had been under constant attack by the Burmese. There he built a new temple, Wat Pra Kaeo, and brought the Emerald Buddha to be enshrined there. Royal chronicles state that it was during this time that the name of Luang Prabang, City of the Golden Buddha, to honour the image, came into usage, replacing the earlier town's name of Muang Swa. The Burmese, under King Bayinnaung, also attacked Lan Na and Setthathirat relinquished his claim to that throne. They then attacked Vientiane which came under Burmese control for seven years. Setthathirat died mysteriously, having vanished during a campaign in Attapeu in 1574, and eventually Luang Prabang and Vientiane were united under King Nokeo Kumman, 1591-96. Several more kings reigned until King Sulinya Vongsa ushered in an era of peace and a golden age, between 1637-1694. Luang Prabang's influence spread to Siam and Cambodia. During his reign, the first Europeans visited Laos, in particular Gerrit van Wuysthoff, a Dutch merchant, in 1641-42, and an Italian Jesuit missionary, G.M. Leris, between 1642-48. The former described his visit in a detailed account, while Leris's descriptions were written down by a fellow Jesuit, G.F. de Marini. One of the few early descriptions of this remote kingdom, it was published in Italian, then French, and alluded to the considerable riches and power of the Lao kingdom, the splendour of the royal court and the religious ceremonies.

Statue of King Setthathirat in front of Phra That Luang, Vientiane. During the Phra That Luang festival, rice balls are placed in the niches of the wall as a way of paying respect to the king's spirit.

Sulinya Vongsa prudently arranged an alliance with Annam, in present day Vietnam, by wedding the daughter of the emperor Le Thanh Ton. Demarcated frontiers were created with Vietnam, and it was decreed that those people living in houses on stilts owed allegiance to Sulinya Vongsa, whereas those occupying houses built on the ground were subjects of the Dai Viet.

After his death in 1694, Lane Xang, at a disadvantage because it had no coastal trading area, split into three kingdoms: Luang Prabang, Vientiane and Champassak, a new kingdom in the south. Luang Prabang, ruled by Sulinya's grandson, became linked to China, while Vientiane, ruled by his nephew, was closer to Hué and Hanoi, and Champassak was linked to Siam. Strategically located, Laos formed a buffer zone between China, Vietnam and Siam, and in the 1700s there were incessant wars with Siam, leading to Siamese domination of the Lao world.

In 1774, a treaty of alliance was signed and Luang Prabang became a vassal state of Siam. The Siamese seized the Pra Bang Buddha and carried it off in 1728. Although the image was returned, it was seized again in 1778, along with the Emerald Buddha, and taken to Bangkok. While the Pra Bang image was brought back in 1867, its presence having been blamed for a series of droughts, the Emerald Buddha remained in Bangkok. The Pra Bang was returned to Wat Visoun, but after the monastery was destroyed, it was installed in Wat Mai from 1897 until 1947.

Luang Prabang continued to maintain alliances with Lan Na, Chiang Mai and Sipsong Pan Na. Conflict remained between Vientiane and Bangkok, however, and in 1828 the Siamese attacked and absorbed Vientiane into their territory. Both Luang Prabang and Vientiane were influenced by Siamese culture which was starting to become Europeanised. In Luang Prabang European goods began to be available in the markets. However, Siamese domination eventually gave way to the French annexation of Lao territories and new influences.

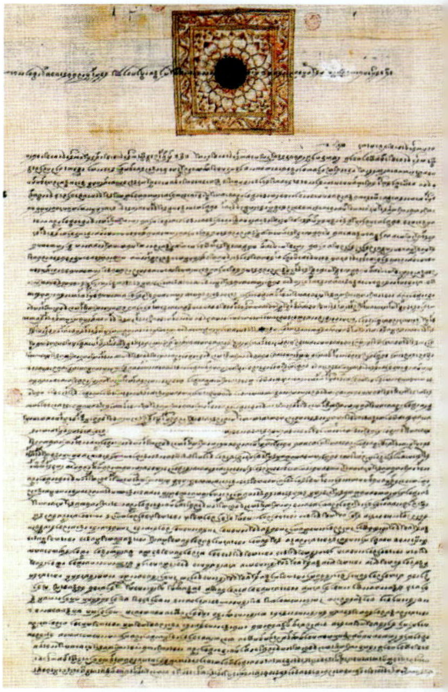

Royal charter on cloth of the kings of Vieng Chen and Luang Prabang from 17th to 18th centuries. (Courtesy The National Library of Thailand)

An etching of Henri Mouhot in the forests of Laos.

M. Henri Mouhot. — Dessin de H. Rousseau d'après une photographie.

Henri Mouhot

In 1861, the intrepid French explorer and naturalist Henri Mouhot (1826-1861) arrived in the town, in the wake of his exploration in Cambodia and 'discovery' of the temples of Angkor in 1860. His diaries, published posthumously, extolled the beauty of Luang Prabang with its numerous temples Mouhot was a real Victorian polymath, a naturalist, botanist, entomologist, ethnologist, philologist, zoologist, linguist and conchologist, as well as a gifted artist and writer. He recorded everything he found with inspiring drawings and prose. Resident in Jersey, he was married to Annette, a descendent of Mungo Park. He became interested in the 'land beyond Siam' and went there under the auspices of the Royal Geographical Society, but at his own expense. He travelled through Laos with half a dozen elephants, covering about 13 miles a day through the jungle, and completed a journey of 500 miles, from the borders of Laos to Luang Prabang.

On 25 July, 1861, he reached Luang Prabang, and wrote about the "delightful little town, set in its amphitheatre of mountains – if it were not for the blazing heat, it would be a paradise." He was welcomed by King Chantarath (r. 1851-72).

Mouhot then travelled on, intending to reach China, but by October 1861 he had caught malaria. Feverish and weak, he decided to turn back to Luang Prabang, but never got there. He wrote his last diary entry on 29 October and on 10 November 1861 died, by the Nam Khan river, five miles east of Luang Prabang. His guides buried him there and carried his diaries back to Bangkok, where they were later published as *Travels in Siam, Cambodia and Laos.* At his grave a colonial-style tomb was erected in 1867 by the French Commander Doudart de Lagrée. Then, like Angkor, it became overgrown and forgotten until rediscovered in 1990 by a French writer, Jean-Michel Strobino, with the help of a Laotian guide, Monkhol Sasorith. As a result, Mouhot's birthplace, the town of Montbéliard, in France, donated a plaque, and the French government agreed to a grant for its upkeep. (See page 158)

An etching of Mouhot sitting on the floor paying respect to the king who sits on the raised platform. (RB)

Left: *Auguste Pavie, in a white suit, holding a black hat, was the leader of the French expedition to Luang Prabang in 1867.*

Below: *Luang Prabang royal seal.*

Bottom: *Pavie's paper written during his trip and sent to France.* (Courtesy Archives of the Ministry of Foreign Affairs, Paris)

Mouhot was followed in 1867 by Doudart de Lagrée's expedition, charting the course of the Mekong, one of the most important explorations of trade routes between Yunnan and the Vietnam Delta. Following the river upstream from the Delta, they covered 9,960 kilometres, and 'discovered' 5,060 kilometres for the first time, producing the Mekong Exploration Commission Report of 1866-1868. The expedition halted in Luang Prabang where they stayed for one month. They produced maps and engravings in the course of their geographical research, many of them veritable works of art, providing further information for France's expansion into Indochina. One of the principal members of the team, the naval officer Francis Garnier, killed in Hanoi in 1873, also praised the lovely setting of the town.

King Sisavangvong. In 1947 he granted a constitution and transformed Laos into a democratic nation for a brief period of time.

Then the French mission arrived, headed by Auguste Pavie, an explorer and diplomat. In 1886 he became the first French vice-consul. He loved Luang Prabang, and quickly learned to speak Lao, as well as Khmer, Thai and Vietnamese. Pavie brought Laos under French control in 1893, but his avowed aim was to 'conquérir les coeurs' (conquer hearts), as he himself had been conquered by the culture and people he found. Under the auspices of the Mission Pavie, numerous French expeditions were conducted by teams of prominent researchers who drew up maps, compiled new historical and scientific information and studied the natural history of the area, focusing especially on the disputed borders of Laos, Siam, Cambodia, Yunnan and Vietnam, and thereby assisting France's colonial interests.

The French always kept the Lao monarchs on the throne and encouraged a grand court style, formal and traditional, fixing the Luang Prabang court in a historical time and context. An old black and white photograph of King Oun Kham and his courtiers shows the monarch on a raised seven-tiered throne, decked out in silken finery, wearing a tall pointed crown, with tiered umbrellas overhead, brocade fans and kneeling attendants. His son King Sisavangvong (r. 1905-1959), was also photographed wearing a lavish brocaded silk shirt, a *chong kraben,* stockings and embroidered slippers. Yet, simultaneously in Bangkok, King Rama V was photographed in a European three piece suit and overcoat, with a bow tie, wing collars, black top hat and patent leather pumps, sporting an English walking stick.

Although this courtly pomp flattered the royals, their political power diminished, becoming the domain of the French colonisers, who employed a bureaucracy of educated Vietnamese. But they continued to support the monarchy, even building the new palace in Luang Prabang in the early 1900s, a blend of French and Lao architecture. They also succeeded in inculcating notions of French superiority and sophistication to the extent that the sons of King Sisavangvong and the Lao élite were all educated in France.

Statue of Sisavangvong in the palace grounds in front of the royal theatre.

King Oun Kham of Luang Phrabang and the Crown Prince Chao Sakharine and Chao Oupahat Boun Khong. In the center is the young Prince Sisavangvong. (RB)

Left: *King Sakharine and his wife. His father, King Oun Kham, gave up the throne in favour of Sakharine in 1889.* (RB)

Prince Phetsarath declared independence from France and was elected the first prime minister of Laos in 1945.

The colonial government was, however, an economic failure. Grant Evans in *A Short History of Laos* writes that it "raised just enough money to pay its officials and no more. There was nothing for development, road building, schools, hospitals, or any of the other fruits of the *mission civilisatrice.*" Finance came from sources such as trade in opium. Indeed, the French encouraged opium growing among the Hmong in northern Laos right up until World War II.

In 1940, France's Vichy government signed the Matsuoka-Henry Pact allowing Japan to station troops in Indochina. While this recognised Japan's role in Southeast Asia, it maintained France's sovereignty in the region. However, the French administration was then ousted by the Japanese in March 1945 and they surrendered in August.

This provoked the start of an independence movement in Laos, led by Prince Phetsarath Ratanavongsa (1890-1959), known as the 'iron man of Laos,' prime minister between 1942-45. His father was Prince Boun Khong (1887-1920), an *Oupahat,* or viceroy, a tradition in Laos whereby brothers of a king acted as deputy kings. Boun Khong had 11 sons and 13 daughters by 11 wives. Phetsarath was half brother of the Princes Souvannaphouma and Souvannouvong who became important political figures, but all three espoused different political creeds.

Phetsarath was born in Luang Prabang, second son of Boun Khong and his second wife Princess Thongsy, and studied in Saigon and Paris. He returned to Laos in 1912 and married Princess Nhin Kham Venne. He worked for the French governor in Vientiane and in 1919 was given the title of Somdeth Chao

Oupahat Boun Khong with his eleven wives and daughters. (RB)

The pro-communist leader of the Pathet Laos party, Prince Souvannouvong.

Ratsaphakhinay, a title held by his father and one of the highest ranks in the country. He was Director of Indigenous Affairs of Laos and as the country's last *Oupahat* became a leading figure, establishing the system of ranks and titles of the civil service, the administrative system of the Buddhist clergy, the Institute of Law and Administration and creating the judicial system.

When the Japanese invaded, occupying Laos for six months, they imprisoned French officials and confiscated their property. Phetsarath left Vientiane for Luang Prabang to be with King Sisavangvong whom the Japanese had encouraged to declare independence. Sisavangvong felt that Laos was too small to be independent and although he was forced to agree, his loyalty to the French remained. The French later returned and occupied Laos.

In 1946 Phetsarath, who supported his brother Souvannaphouma, a neutralist and democrat, became leader of the Lao Issara, an anti-French revolutionary movement for independence, thus bringing him into conflict with King Sisavangvong. Consequently Phetsarath moved to Thailand for 11 years, where he headed the Lao Issara government-in-exile, living with a Thai consort, Mom Aphiphorn. During this period, Lao politics were dominated by the Princes Souvannaphouma and Souvanouvong, with Phetsarath mediating between the two.

Souvannouvong became known as the 'Red Prince'. Born in 1912, he was the son of Boun Khong's 11th wife, and younger than his two half brothers. Having studied in France, he married a Vietnamese woman and subsquently fought against colonialism and supported communism and Vietnam.

Souvannaphouma, born in 1901, became one of the greatest statesman of Laos. He was educated in France and, like all the princes, was French in manner and tastes – apparently they all appreciated fine wines and cigars. He was an engineer in Laos on his return and supported the 1945 declaration of independence made by King Sisavangvong under the Japanese. But when French troops returned to Laos, he joined the Lao Issara in Thailand. Following partial independence, Souvannaphouma headed an American-backed Royal Lao Government of Independent Laos, a divided country, until 1954. For the next 20 years Souvannaphouma dominated Lao politics as the United States became increasingly involved.

Souvannaphouma strived for democracy in Laos. (RB)

Souvannouvong, meanwhile, led the Pathet Lao, the communist party, with Vietnamese backing, and when Souvannaphouma became Prime Minister in 1956 he tried to integrate them into a coalition government.

In 1957, Phetsarath returned to Laos, was received by King Sisavangvong and reinstated as *Oupahat* of the Kingdom. Phetsarath visited Sam Neua and Phong Saly where Souvannouvong symbolically offered the return of the Pathet Lao's two provinces to the Kingdom of Laos. He then remained in his Villa Xiengkeo in Luang Prabang.

Phetsarath became an accomplished astrologer and astronomer. It is said that his fascination with the subjects started on a visit to England, during his residence in France, when he stayed in Brighton where his landlord introduced him to astronomy.

Phetsarath later wrote a treatise on Lao astrology and reformed the Lao calendar, which is half solar and half lunar. The Lao still work on Phetsarath's principles today. He also instigated the museum in Wat Visoun, bringing numerous historic Buddha images to be stored there. In 1959 he suffered a brain haemorrhage and died, aged 69. He is revered in Laos to this day.

In 1959 Crown Prince Savang Vatthana became regent and his father Sisavangvong died two months later. A grand funeral was held in early 1961. Prince Savang Vatthana, the last, uncrowned king, had attended the Écoles des Sciences Politiques in Paris. Peace loving, he read French literature, especially Proust, and it was said that he could recite by heart whole chapters of *A La Recherche du Temps Perdu.* But the royal family's role in Laos was drawing to a close as the political situation became increasingly complex.

The last crown prince of Laos, Savang Vatthana. (RB)

During the 1960s and1970s civil war erupted, involving Vietnamese, Chinese and American backed forces and various *coups d'etat*. As the shadow of the Vietnam War fell across Laos, it became known as the 'other theatre'. A nine year 'secret war' led by the US Central Intelligence Agency was waged over Laos. They recruited 60,000 Hmong mercenaries, some just teenagers, led by Hmong General Vang Pao, to fight the Vietnamese Communists. The Ho Chi Minh trail, a jungle clad network of paths along the border with Vietnam, was used for supplying Communist units in South Vietnam and Cambodia, and was repeatedly bombed. The Plain of Jars became a strategic area, with secret airbases for the CIA's airline Air America. B52 bombers flying out from Guam unloaded bombs against the Ho Chi Minh trail and after sorties over North Vietnam dropped their unexploded bombs on Laos. About 1,100,000 tons of bombs fell on the Ho Chi Minh Trail and 500,000 tons on northern Laos, a greater tonnage than was dropped on Germany in World War II, making Laos one of the most heavily bombed nations on earth. An estimated 30,000 Hmong died.

In 1975, the communist Pathet Lao took over. Some 400,000 Lao people fled across the Mekong to Thailand including many Hmong. Souvannouvong became President and Kaysone Phomivane became Secretary General of the Lao People's Revolutionary Party on 2 December. Souvannaphouma helped with the transfer of power, but his role diminished. He died in January 1984. Souvannouvong died in January 1995, in Vientiane.

Savang Vatthana was removed from the palace in Luang Prabang with his family and they subsequently perished in the hills of Xam Neua, around the Plain of Jars. According to Christopher Kremmer's book *Bamboo Palace,* Savang Vatthana died in March 1980, his wife Queen Kham Phoui in 1982 and Crown Prince Vongsavang in January 1980. The palace was turned into a museum.

Hmong boys employed by the Central Intelligence Agency (CIA) of the United States to fight in the 'secret war' in Laos.

Kings of Lane Xang

Fa Ngum	1353-73
Sam Saentai	1373-1416
Lan Kham Deng,	1416-27
Phommathat	1428-29
Mun Sai	1430
Fa Khai	1430-33
Kong Kham	1433-34
Yukhon	1434-35
Kham Keut	1435-38
Sao Takaphat	1438-79
Theng Kham	1479-86
Lasenthai	1486-96
Som Phu	1496-1501
Visounnarat	1501-20
Photthisarat	1520-48
(Sai) Setthathirat	1548-71
Sensulinthara	1571-75
Maha Upahat	1575-80
Sensulinthara	1580-81
Nakhon Noi	1582-83
Interregnum	1583-91
Nokeo Kumman	1591-96
Thammikrat	1596-1622
Upanyuvarat	1622-23
Photthisarat	1623-27
Mon Keo	1627
Upanyuvarat *unstable period*	
Ton Kham	
Visai	
Sulinya Vongsa	1637-94

Kings of Luang Prabang

Kithsarat	1707-25
Khamon Noi	1726-27
Inta Som	1727-76
Sotika Kuman	1776-81
Vong	1781-87
Interregnum	1787-91
Anourat	1791-1817
Manthatourat	1817-36
Sukaseum	1836-51
Chantarath	1851-72
Oun Kham	1872-87
Interregnum	1887-94
Sakharine (also known as Zakarinth)	1894-1904
Sisavangvong	1904-59
Savang Vatthana (also known as Sisavang Vatthana) (not crowned)	1959-75

Where historical dates are at variance, it should be remembered that the Laotian calendar, originally based on Hinduism and Buddhism, belongs to the luni-solar system. Thus, a lunar year is 11 days shorter than a solar year, and the years correspond to the Buddhist rather than the Gregorian calendar. Cyclical years are important when checking historical dates. In principle, if the date given does not accord with the 60 year cycle, then it is incorrect.

Current flag of the Lao PDR.

Flag of the former kingdom Lane Xang.

The Lao People's Democratic Republic is still one of the world's poorest countries with an economy based primarily on subsistence farming. Since adopting the New Economic Mechanism in 1986, economic activity from a central command system has been transformed to a market-based approach. Economic growth has accelerated as a result. The opening of the Friendship Bridge across the Mekong in 1994 has fostered relations with Thailand, as have subsequent bridges in 2007 and 2011, while a fourth Thai-Lao Friendship Bridge has been proposed. Laos was admitted to the World Trade Organisation in 2012. Tourism has become an important industry, focusing on cultural and ecological tourism.

Luang Prabang's aura of idyllic serenity is, in reality, as misleading as its history is one of constant warfare.

The Lao Flag

The Lao PDR flag became official with the creation of the republic in 1975. The white circle symbolises sunrise over the Mekong river. It is also said to represent unity after the struggles for independence. This flag represents a communist country without having any symbolic stars or hammer and sickle.

Opposite: *Current map of Lao PDR.*

CHINA
VIETNAM
ANMAR
Phongsali
Muang Sing
Boten
Luang Namtha
Oudom Xai
Houei Xai
Vieng Kham
Xam Neua
Na Meo
LOAS
Luang Prabang
Xieng Ngeun
Xayaboury (Sayabouli)
Phonsavan
Plain of Jars
Nong Het
Nam Kanh
Highest Mountain
Xaysomboune
Vang Vieng
Gulf of Tonkin
Mekong
Nam Phao
Vientiane
Nong Khai
Na Phao
Nakhon Phanom
Thakek
Khammouane
Nam Phao
Dene savanh
Mukdahan
Savannakhet
Xayphouthong
THAILAND
Salavan
Paksé
Chong Mek
Champasak
Attapeu
Vat Phou
Sanamxai
N
0 10 20 30 km
Khong
Cambodia
authorized border crossing
CAMBODIA
Mekong

Art and Religion

"A beautiful soul is better than a beautiful form." Lao saying

The art of Laos is entirely religious and is expressed in the proliferation of Buddhist temples. The temple is the fundamental structure of religious life and is central to its concepts, incorporating symbols of the sacred mountain, orientation to the four cardinal points and a demarcated area for rituals, festivals and sacred traditions. However, although Buddhist, the temples of Luang Prabang also incorporate Hindu imagery as well as animistic traditions. Hinduism preceded Buddhism in the region, while animism is the archaic belief system of the Lao, as it is for many of the people of Southeast Asia.

In Lao mythology the earth was covered with primeval forests and *phi,* the spirits or soul of the mountains, rivers, trees and streams. Rice has many spirits, not only in the grains but in the whole plant and thereby in the entire rice field. Various prayers and festivals, still performed today, protect the *phi* of the rice and ensure abundant crops and good harvests. Other *phi,* both benevolent and malevolent, were placated by special ceremonies throughout the year. Myths, especially cosmogonic (those describing the creation of the universe) ones, were of primary importance, for they related directly with people's very existence. They told how the king of the heavenly gods, Khun Borom, descended to earth to become the monarch, so henceforth kings were considered holy as well. The royal tutelary gods, the *devata luang,* of Luang Prabang were Pu No and Na No, spirits which protected the area, and their recreated images are still incorporated into celebrations every year. So "myth and history blended and fused," as Betty Gosling writes in *Old Luang Prabang,* and the surrounding ceremonies and rites perpetuated Luang Prabang as a royal city.

The annual Pu No and Na No Dance at Wat Visoun. This ritual invokes the spirits of the region and shows the survival of animistic beliefs within a Buddhist community. (Courtesy University of Illinois)

When Hinduism and Buddhism came to Southeast Asia in the 3rd and 4th centuries AD, brought by Indian merchants, these religions were adopted by local people and incorporated into their existing traditions. Syncretism, the combining of different belief systems, is a fundamental part of spiritual life for Lao people. They absorbed Hinduism and Buddhism principally from the Khmers whose empire extended beyond Cambodia into Laos.

Buddhism had spread from India in the centuries following the life of the historical Buddha, Prince Siddharta Gautama, born there in 543 BC. After encountering scenes of suffering such as disease, poverty and death, he abandoned his palace and family to seek the truth. For six years he became an extreme ascetic, but rejecting this path, chose instead what he called the Middle Way. He finally attained enlightenment – Buddha means 'enlightened one' – in Bodh Gaya, while meditating under a banyan tree, *Ficus religiosa,* often known as a *bodhi* tree.

Opposite: *Wooden Buddha statues gilded with gold leaf standing inside Wat Visoun. Collections of Buddha images are a common sight in many of the sanctuaries of Luang Prabang.*

In important temples, almost every inch of the wall is covered with images. Above in Wat Mai, stencil and small Buddha amulets are used to decorate the entire wall.

He preached that there were Four Noble Truths that had the power to liberate human beings from the endless cycle of death and rebirth (*samsara*): that all life is suffering, suffering is caused by desire, the cessation of desire will bring peace, and the end of suffering is achieved by following the Eightfold Path. He founded a community of monks who learned to follow the path and who recorded his sermons. The Wheel of the Law symbolised his doctrine and teaching which incorporated theories about *samsara,* and *karma,* the cause and effect of moral acts accumulated in this and former lives. He encouraged the acquisition of wisdom and taught that meditation lay at the heart of Buddhist practice.

Buddhism split into different strands as its influence radiated out across Asia, evolving within different cultures and harmonising with existing traditions. Theravada Buddhism, 'the doctrine of the elders', or the so-called 'lesser vehicle', took the southern route through Sri Lanka to Southeast Asia and became the dominant form of Buddhism in Laos.

Buddhism was adopted in Luang Prabang in the 13th and early 14th centuries. It spread slowly and was first declared a state religion in the 14th century by King Fa Ngum, which he did by accepting from his Khmer father-in-law the golden Pra Bang Buddha, the palladium of the Kingdom of Lane Xang. In 1356 he built a *wat* in Muang Sawa (the early name of Luang Prabang) to house this revered image. During King Sulinya Vongsa's reign in the mid-17th century, Buddhism was taught in schools. It adopted some forms of *phi* worship, whereby sacred images of Buddhism were surrounded by ritual offerings of food, fruits, incense and candles, in the animistic tradition, as they still are today. Such offerings and rites were also accorded to the dead so that their souls or ghosts would not remain near the living.

Theravada Buddhism stresses three principal aspects of existence: suffering; impermanence and transiency; and non-essentiality of reality. It teaches that the path to enlightenment is achieved by individual effort, and is most accessible by joining the monkhood. The other form of Buddhism, Mahayana, the 'greater vehicle', adhered to in East Asia, is less rigorous. Mahayan Buddhists believe in *bodhisattvas,* enlightened beings with compassion who, in order to assist man, delay entry into *nirvana,* literally the absence of all that is, the transcendence of the delusory world and freedom from the process of birth, disease, old age and death. In contrast, Theravada Buddhists recognise only the Buddha as a *bodhisattva.*

Iconography in Lao temples shows *bodhisattvas* in illustrations of the previous incarnations of the historical Buddha, the *Jataka* tales, which relate his 547 lives before he was born as Prince Siddharta Gautama and achieved enlightenment. The final ten *jataka* tales, especially the last one, the *Vessantara Jataka,* the Great Birth Tale, in which the Buddha was born as Prince Vessantara, are the most important and feature in much Lao art and literature. The *jataka* tales focus on the Buddha's moral evolution, his pursuit of virtues, the *paramitas,* and his inner strength. They illuminate the most essential virtue in Buddhism.

the act of giving, *dana* in Pali. In addition, local folklore and legends are often incorporated into these images.

The practice of painting and sculpture accompanied Buddhist beliefs from India across Asia, reinforcing the fundamental tenets of the philosophy. Ceremonial halls and stupas (*stup* is Sanskrit for accumulate or gather together) were built to house objects for worship and meditation. In early imagery the Buddha was never portrayed, but was suggested by symbols such as stupas, footprints, the *bodhi* tree, or the *dharma* wheel, symbolising the preaching of the first sermon in the Deer Garden. The repetition of such images was considered auspicious.

Buddha statues in bhumisparsa mudra *signify the moment just before the Buddha attained enlightenment.*

Imagery which included the Buddha, and *bodhisattvas,* originated in Gandhara, present-day Pakistan, the frontier region of India where sculpture became influenced by Hellenism. Alexander the Great had colonised the far north-west of India for two years from 327 BC and established a Greek trading empire. Greek art, like Roman art, created images of gods which embodied perfect human beauty and Indian artists emulated them. Early Gandharan sculptures of the Buddha imbued Buddhist art with a highly refined aesthetic sense that was a fusion of Indian art and Greek classicism. Buddhist art developed in the Gupta and post-Gupta period, centred on the north Indian plains, between the 5th-10th centuries AD, considered the classical period of India's history. Subsequently, the most inspiring work was in Sri Lanka and then in the great Khmer Empire of the 9th-15th centuries, as well as in Champa, in Vietnam, and Sukhothai, in Thailand.

Eventually, the vocabulary of Buddhist iconography would include the 32 special attributes with which the figure of the Buddha was endowed, such as the *ushnisha,* the protruberance on the top of his head, and the *urna,* the mark between his eyebrows, or his hair curled stylistically in a clockwise direction. Long earlobes denoted royalty, as the Buddha would have worn heavy earrings during his princely life. The three incised lines on the neck are signs of beauty, while his fingers were all of equal length. The Buddha's robe is another important part of the iconography, and some statues have a nimbus, a halo, around the body. The figure is represented in one of the six poses, *mudras,* or ritual gestures. *Abhaya,* is the pose of giving reassurance, with the right hand held out; *Bhumisparsa,* touching the earth to call the earth goddess to witness his enlightenment; *Dharmachakra* turning the Wheel of Law, the hand held in front of the chest; *Dhyana,* the attitude of meditation, the right hand in front of the chest; *Vara,* giving benediction; *Vitarka,* the gesture of preaching and giving a sermon, with one hand or both hands held outwards.

Lao Buddha, Vientiane. Note the indigenous facial features.

In the art of Laos, the Buddha was depicted standing with hands raised calling for peace, *abhaya mudra,* standing with hands by his side 'calling for rain', *hiek fone,* walking, seated in the lotus

position for meditation, *vajrasana,* calling the earth to witness, *bhumisparsa mudra,* or reclining to symbolise the Buddha's passing into *nirvana.*

Stylistically, images of the Buddha in Lao art evolved through several stages. At first the artists, who were always anonymous, copied past Khmer and Lan Na (northern Thailand) styles. Madeleine Giteau, in her book *The Art of Laos,* reinforces the point that artists did not create naturalistic representations of the Buddha, but modelled a stylised image inspired by sacred texts. Tall, slender figures were sculpted in idealised representations that were deeply spiritual and yet, at the same time, human in their portrayal of delicate sensibilities. Thus the depiction of the Buddha passing into *nirvana* could be understood by the viewer.

Gradually sculptors developed their own artistic vocabulary, with expressive eyes that contributed to the emotional content, radiating compassion, looking down to the supplicant or meditating, with a sharply defined, triangular-shaped aquiline nose, completely flat underneath and carefully incised, often bearing similarity to the features of Lao people themselves. The later statues, with their slender forms and graceful arms, exude fluidity and refinement. In Lao imagery, the Buddha's outer robe, the *uttarasanga*, is shown open over the left shoulder and often transparent or sheer, as if to let the luminosity and superhuman nature of the Buddha's body shine through.

The Buddha is sometimes shown with ceremonial emblems and regalia, placed upon an elevated pedestal. The pedestal in Lao sculpture is a tall superimposed plinth, broad at the base, and becoming taller and taller, narrowing as it reaches the top. While symbolic of the ascent towards the heavens, this elongated form adds a flowing grace to Lao sculpture.

Images of Rama, hero of the *Phra Lak Phra Lam,* the Lao version of the Indian epic the *Ramayana,* carved on the doors of the *wats* are similarly long and slender, posed like dancers, with delicate features and dignified gestures, attired in princely raiment and radiating sophistication.

Lao folk art includes small, simple Buddha images, usually carved in wood, that are taken to places of pilgrimage such as the Pak Ou caves. There used to be many hundreds of them there, placed as offerings during festivals. As Somkiart Lopetcharat writes in his book *Lao Buddha,* these unpretentious works of folk art have a special charm, which is reinforced by their haphazard placement in pilgrimage sites.

Other sacred imagery found in Lao art includes depictions of the *traiphum,* the three worlds of Buddhist cosmology, heaven, hell and earth. There are three basic perceptions of the world, *samsara,* the continuous series of cycles of existence, *traidhatuka,* the threefold world, and *cakravala,* the configuration of the world with Mount Meru at the centre. The colossal Mount Meru, centre of the universe, surrounded by seven concentric chains of mountains, is the abode of Indra, God of the Sky in Hinduism, or of the celestial Buddha. At the four cardinal points are four

Buddha images in the Pak Ou caves. These sculptures were brought to the cave by villagers during festivals.

Opposite: *Gold stencil on the black exterior wall of Wat Xieng Thong's assembly hall.* (PP)

position for meditation, *vajrasana,* calling the earth to witness, *bhumisparsa mudra,* or reclining to symbolise the Buddha's passing into *nirvana.*

Stylistically, images of the Buddha in Lao art evolved through several stages. At first the artists, who were always anonymous, copied past Khmer and Lan Na (northern Thailand) styles. Madeleine Giteau, in her book *The Art of Laos,* reinforces the point that artists did not create naturalistic representations of the Buddha, but modelled a stylised image inspired by sacred texts. Tall, slender figures were sculpted in idealised representations that were deeply spiritual and yet, at the same time, human in their portrayal of delicate sensibilities. Thus the depiction of the Buddha passing into *nirvana* could be understood by the viewer.

Gradually sculptors developed their own artistic vocabulary, with expressive eyes that contributed to the emotional content, radiating compassion, looking down to the supplicant or meditating, with a sharply defined, triangular-shaped aquiline nose, completely flat underneath and carefully incised, often bearing similarity to the features of Lao people themselves. The later statues, with their slender forms and graceful arms, exude fluidity and refinement. In Lao imagery, the Buddha's outer robe, the *uttarasanga,* is shown open over the left shoulder and often transparent or sheer, as if to let the luminosity and superhuman nature of the Buddha's body shine through.

Buddha images in the Pak Ou caves. These sculptures were brought to the cave by villagers during festivals.

The Buddha is sometimes shown with ceremonial emblems and regalia, placed upon an elevated pedestal. The pedestal in Lao sculpture is a tall superimposed plinth, broad at the base, and becoming taller and taller, narrowing as it reaches the top. While symbolic of the ascent towards the heavens, this elongated form adds a flowing grace to Lao sculpture.

Images of Rama, hero of the *Phra Lak Phra Lam,* the Lao version of the Indian epic the *Ramayana,* carved on the doors of the *wats* are similarly long and slender, posed like dancers, with delicate features and dignified gestures, attired in princely raiment and radiating sophistication.

Lao folk art includes small, simple Buddha images, usually carved in wood, that are taken to places of pilgrimage such as the Pak Ou caves. There used to be many hundreds of them there, placed as offerings during festivals. As Somkiart Lopetcharat writes in his book *Lao Buddha,* these unpretentious works of folk art have a special charm, which is reinforced by their haphazard placement in pilgrimage sites.

Other sacred imagery found in Lao art includes depictions of the *traiphum,* the three worlds of Buddhist cosmology, heaven, hell and earth. There are three basic perceptions of the world, *samsara,* the continuous series of cycles of existence, *traidhatuka,* the threefold world, and *cakravala,* the configuration of the world with Mount Meru at the centre. The colossal Mount Meru, centre of the universe, surrounded by seven concentric chains of mountains, is the abode of Indra, God of the Sky in Hinduism, or of the celestial Buddha. At the four cardinal points are four

Opposite: *Gold stencil on the black exterior wall of Wat Xieng Thong's assembly hall.* (PP)

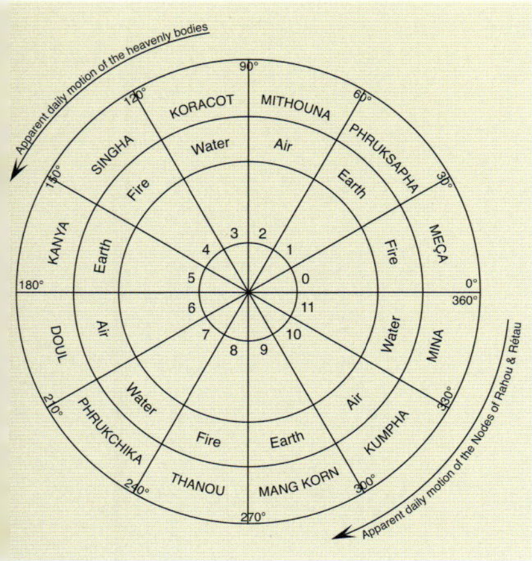

Laotian zodiac.

guardian rulers and 33 gods. In addition, Buddhism absorbed the astrological elements of the eight planets, the 12 zodiac houses and the 28 lunar mansions, believing that the world rests on four primary elements, earth, water, wind and space.

The lotus is a recurring image. Its origins are in Hindu mythology which holds the lotus as sacred, symbolising in the *yoni,* the female generative organ, and thus the origin of life. The spirit of the Supreme Being was personified by a golden lotus on a vast sea. Brahma, God of Creation, representative of the Universe, was born from a golden lotus. Sculptures of Vishnu, the Preserver, often show him in a cosmic sleep on the mythical serpent Ananta, dreaming in new worlds, while from his navel issues the golden lotus on a long stalk from which Brahma was born. Its petals expand into the universe and from them arise hills, mountains and valleys. The lotus appears as a pedestal or throne to support many images both in Hinduism and Buddhism. The Buddha was associated with the lotus at his birth, and is often depicted standing on one. That its roots are in water and its petals above is symbolic of the stages of wisdom and knowledge.

The *naga,*or *nyak,* the mythical multi-headed serpent, is another ever-present motif in Lao art that is also associated with water. Serpents were revered as spirits of the rivers, as water had both destructive and life-giving powers, especially in countries such as Laos where water management was less sophisticated. The origins of *nagas* in Lao mythology probably date back to the influence of the Khmer, where images of the Buddha sheltered by the *naga* Muchalinda were prevalent. Similarly, the *naga* bridges of Khmer temples have been transformed into the *naga* stairways that form the entrances to Buddhist temples. The shape of Luang Prabang itself resembles a *naga*, according to legend, and is one of the reasons it was chosen as the sacred royal capital.

As well as Hindu and Buddhist symbols, the 12 animals of the zodiac – the rat, the ox, the tiger, the rabbit, the dragon, the snake, the horse, the goat, the monkey, the cock, the dog and the pig – appear in Lao imagery. These reflect the 12 years of the lunar cycle.

Monasteries were important respositeries of knowledge. Manuscripts on palm leaf, in Pali, taught the Buddhist canon. Housed in scripture cabinets, they were wrapped in textiles, which resonate with religious symbolism. Usually woven by women in the royal court, they had animistic and Buddhist iconography and incorporated anthropomorphic figures and symbolic diagrams, *yantra,* to ward off evil spirits.

Manuscript box usually kept in the library in temple compound as the manuscript is the heart of the Buddha's teaching.

Over the last ten years, the manuscript holdings of more than 800 monasteries have been surveyed by The Lao Manuscripts Programme and approximately 86,000 texts preserved and a central data pool created. Microfilms taken of about 12,000 selected texts are now incorporated in the Digital Library of Lao Manuscripts Collection, based at the National Museum of Laos in Vientiane.

Three categories of texts make up the Buddhist canon: the *tripitaka,* the *sutras* and the *vinaya.* The *tripitaka,* or 'three

baskets', is the primary text for Theravada Buddhism, written in Pali and derived from oral sources. It is divided, as the name suggests, into three parts, incorporating the teachings of the Buddha, his discourses and the organisation of Buddhist communities. The *sutras* (*sutra* literally means string or thread) are the sermons of the historical Buddha transcribed in Sanskrit or Pali several centuries after his death. They describe where and when the Buddha was preaching and contain parables designed to edify the listener. The *vinaya* set forth the rules and regulations of monastic life such as dress and eating habits. In addition, *abhidarma,* another category, are philosophical and psychological discussions and interpretations by monks and scholars.

The most important secular text, *Phra Lak Phra Lam*, is based on the 48,000 line Hindu epic, the *Ramayana*. It follows the original story but places it in a Lao landscape. In the *Ramayana*, Rama a prince of Ayodhya, an *avatar,* or reincarnation of Vishnu, son of King Dasaratha, marries Princess Sita. Rama is forced to flee into exile with Sita and his brother Laksmana. Sita is abducted by the evil ten-headed demon king Ravana, forcing Rama to go to war against the demons of Langka. With the help of Hanuman, the monkey general, son of the god Vayu, and the monkey army sent by the monkey king Sugriva, he defeats them and wins back Sita. In the Lao version the ending where Sita and Rama are reunited and reconciled with the help of the gods is modified, and figures such as Hanuman are more playful and amorous.

Ancient Lao epics such as the *Sinxai*, the masterpiece of classical Lao literature dating from the reign of King Sulinya Vongsa (1637-94) have many, lengthy stories in which the hero is a Bodhisattva and were performed as didactic entertainment, especially at festivals, together with *Mau Lam*, musical recitals. Legends, such as *The Myth of Khun Burôm*, date from the 16th century, describe the origins of the country. Lao literature, written on folding books of mulberry paper, in two scripts, Lao and Tham, included regional oral folk stories and poetry as well as the *jataka* tales. The *Panna-jataka* tales, interpretations of the Indian canonical *jataka* tales, were a principal source of inspiration for Lao literature and may have entered Laos during the 16th century Kingdom of Lane Xang from Chiang Mai and Lanna. The epics and stories were often chanted or read as religious sermons or poems. *Kaun An* was the most popular form of poetry.

These texts and traditions have all been revived today after being temporarily banned by the communist government.

Tak Bat.

The daily alms round allows lay people to make merit and keeps Buddhism alive.

The *Tak Bat*

The ancient Buddhist tradition of *Tak Bat*, the morning alms round, also known in Lao as *Sai Bat*, is practised each day at dawn. Emerging silently from the town's temples, hundreds of barefoot monks in orange robes walk in single file through the streets to collect food from the local people.

The lay community – men, women and children – kneel or sit with bowls of sticky rice to await the monks to whom they will offer it, an act performed in serenity and prayer. By giving, they earn merit and blessings, participating in a living ritual that is practised throughout the country and throughout Southeast Asia.

The *Tak Bat* is a source of admiration by most visitors but has become popular as a tourist attraction with inevitable disruption to religious life. Authorities request that visitors respect it with appropriate behaviour and dress.

A collection of black and white photographs documenting monastic life in Laos for the last 120 years was accumulated by the venerable late Abbot of Luang Prabang, Phra Khamchan Virachitta Maha Thera. Now, thanks to Khamvone Boulyaphonh and German photographer Hans Georg Berger, these have been saved and digitised for the Buddhist Archive of Luang Prabang. They provide a unique historical record of the *Sangha* in Laos, with its ceremonies, rituals and daily practice. Between 2011-2015 another project, also involving Hans Berger, is researching the Lao Sangha and Modernity.

Luang Prabang as a UNESCO World Heritage Site

Luang Prabang was inscribed on the UNESCO World Heritage list on 2 December 1995, at the Lao government's request, because it shows evidence of a unique combination of nature and architecture, an important crossing point of cultural influences on developments in architecture, arts, monuments and town planning. UNESCO described it thus: "Luang Prabang represents, to an exceptional extent, the successful fusion of the traditional architectural and urban structures and those of the European colonial rulers of the 19th and 20th centuries. Its unique townscape is remarkably well preserved, illustrating a key stage in the blending of two distinct cultural traditions."

As a result, a Heritage House was set up in Luang Prabang in 1996, according to UNESCO recommendations. It incorporates several international projects and reports directly to the Minister of Information and Culture. Its role, co-ordinating with the Urban Development Administration Authority of Luang Prabang, is management, conservation and enhancement of the natural, cultural and architectural heritage within the protected area encompassing the old historic city and the banks of both Mekong and Nam Khan rivers. For this purpose, it has a staff of 20 Lao architects and engineers, administrative officers and four foreign advisors, who also train conservation specialists and advise people on renovation of their houses.

Opposite: *Wat Xieng Thong novices.*

Sacred Architecture: Buddhist Temples

Sacred Architecture: Buddhist Temples

"In their wealth and sumptuousness they are probably the loveliest things to which Laotian art has given birth." Henri Marchal

Monks relaxing in their living quarters.

In Laos, as in much of Southeast Asia, religion and society are not separate. Buddhism is part of the way of life and spiritual well-being is essential to personal and universal harmony. A *wat*, or temple, therefore has several functions. It is a site for religious worship, a community centre, a place of education and of healing, and all young Lao men spend at least a few months of their lives as novice monks in a *wat.*

Historically, altars preceded temples, old tutelary shrines where spirits were appeased, and these evolved into religious buildings. In Luang Prabang the *wats* were grouped around the royal residences, built with royal patronage or by affluent individuals, as funding the building of a *wat* gains merit in Buddhism. The king employed master craftsmen and architects, specialists in ivory, wood, gold or silver, carving and stencilling, and monks themselves work as carpenters, sculptors and painters. The upkeep of most *wats,* and that of the monks living within them, is entirely dependent upon donations from the community. But supporting the monastery and giving alms to the monks also brings merit to the donors.

The varied designs of the temples were studied during the French colonial period by a number of eminent French scholars under the auspices of the École Française d'Éxtrême-Orient. Notable among them were Henri Marchal, Henri Parmentier, George Coedès, Madeleine Giteau, Lunet de la Jonquière, Charles Archaimbault and Louis Finot. Parmentier classified them between 1911 and 1927 architectural styles were categorised into three main groups, denoted by region, namely, Luang Prabang, Vientiane and Xieng Khouang. These are identified principally by the roof styles, and sometimes by construction of the *sim* (assembly hall). The Luang Prabang style has a high roof sweeping down in multiple layers. The *sim* is raised on a tiered foundation, and is usually of brick covered in stucco. The Vientiane style has a taller but narrower roof, composed of just one layer. The Xieng Khouang style has a plain, low roof.

Subsequently the temples have been categorised by UNESCO. They have identified four specific styles, based on the layout and supporting pillars, and the position of the Buddha image inside, which they have classified as Luang Prabang Styles I, II, III and Thai Style. Within these classifications there still remains a variety of sizes, types of roof and ornamentation.

In the UNESCO categorisation, Luang Prabang Style I has pillars within the central structure that are higher than those of the supporting periphery, and a covered gallery surrounds the central structure. Inside, the pedestal of the Buddha is separated from the back wall by a gallery. This simpler style includes Wat Mai, Wat Visoun, Wat Pak Khan and Wat That Luang.

Opposite: *The roof structure of an assembly hall. Note the wealth of gold stencil decoration.* (PP)

The multiple layered, sloping Luang Prabang roof style.

In Luang Prabang Style II, the pillars within the central structure are higher than those of the exterior supporting periphery, as in Style I. However, in this category, the building spreads out across four sections, when viewed from the front eastern end, with a verandah leading to the main portico. Inside, the pedestal of the Buddha is attached to the back wall. This more elaborate style includes Wat Xieng Thong, Wat Khili, Wat Choum Khong, Wat Si Boun Houang, Wat Paphane, Wat Sieng Mouan and Wat Sene.

In Luang Prabang Style III the pillars of the central structure are all of the same height, unlike Styles I and II. There are no pillars within the building, and the building spreads out across three to five sections, with a verandah in front. Inside, the pedestal of the Buddha is attached to the back wall, so there is no gallery behind it. This style includes Wat Chom Phet, Wat Pa Phai, Wat Sop, Wat Aham, Wat Meunna, Wat Phone Say, Wat Ho Xieng, Wat Phra Mahathat, Wat Aphay and Wat Nong.

In the Thai Style, the pillars of the main structure are all of the same height, as in Style III. There are no pillars inside the sanctuary and the building extends across three to four closed sections, preceded by a verandah. Although the basic structure is the same as Luang Prabang Style III, the temples are higher and less graceful. These are later constructions, built during the second half of the 19th century. These include Wat Pa Khe and Wat Pa Huak.

The layout of the *wat* reflects its diverse role. It is a collection of buildings within an enclosure, built flat on the ground as opposed to the stilts of traditional secular architecture. The only exceptions are the libraries, present in important *wats,* which

The cloister and sim *of Wat Mai. Note the Luang Prabang layered roof sweeping down almost to the ground.*

Xieng Khouang roof style.

Vientiane roof style.

UNESCO categorisation of temples.

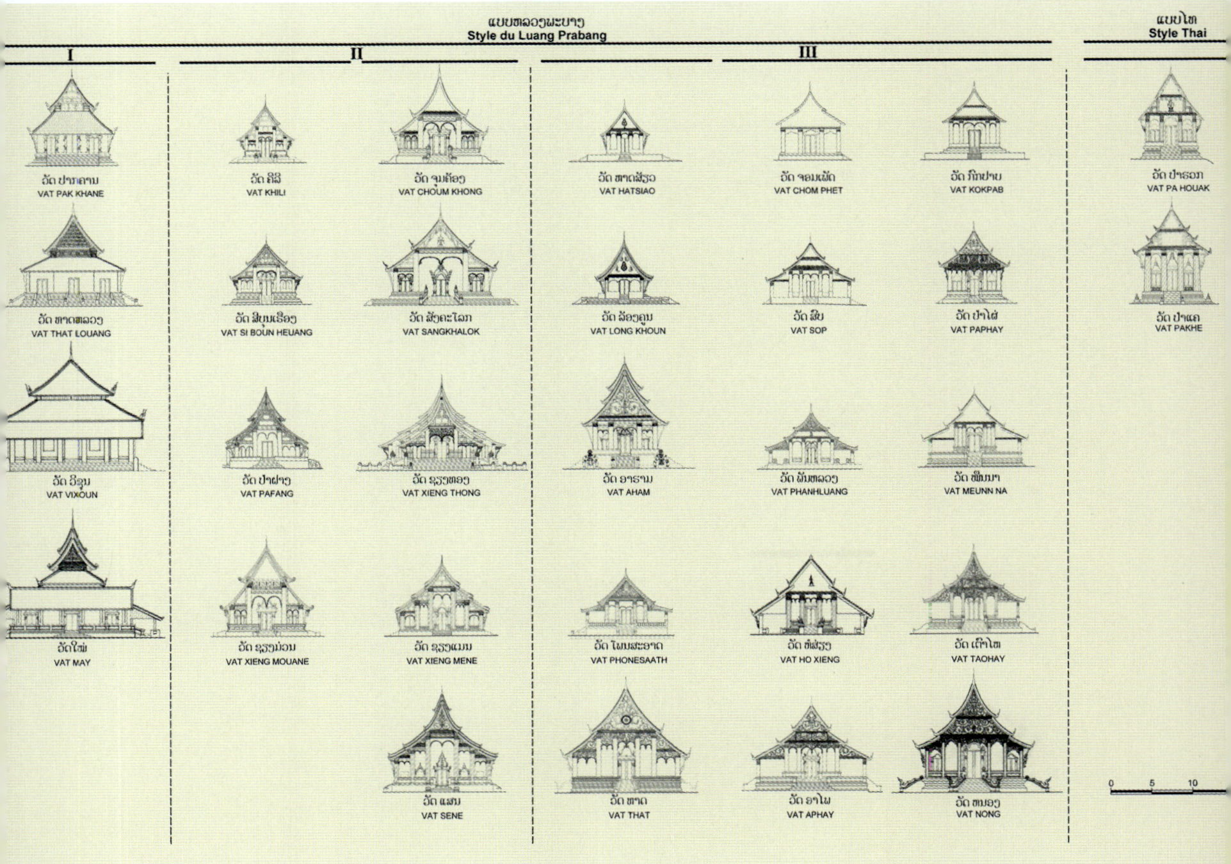

A spirit house just outside a cave temple. (OC)

were sometimes raised on stilts to protect the sacred texts. A *wat* complex is composed of the following: an outer wall or cloister, *phra rabieng;* the monks' living quarters, *kutis;* a sacred library, *hor tai;* stupas, *that,* for relics and ashes; and at the heart of the complex the holiest building, the *sim.* The *sim* is a congregational hall, a place for meditation and meetings, designed to hold laymen and devotees. It faces east, auspiciously, in the direction of the rising sun. The entrance may be guarded by mythical animals, such as lions or *nagas* and a short staircase leading up to the verandah, typically flanked with a balustrade with more *nagas,* their heads rearing up. The drum chapel, *hor kong,* is located away from the main area because it is believed to possess a *phi.* Often a shelter in the complex protects a wooden boat for the annual boat races.

Most temples also have a small spirit house in a corner of the grounds that is associated with the *phi khuan wat,* the benevolent spirit of the *wat.*

The size and proportion of Lao temples have a human scale, which establishes an immediacy of contact between the pilgrim and the sacred space, creating an intimacy where the worshipper is not overawed. Although neither overwhelming or grandiose, these ornate structures give aesthetic pleasure with their understated elegance.

In Theravada Buddhism the concept of an institutional boundary, *sima*, from Pali, is a designated sacred space surrounded with murals. It is within this boundary that the *sanghakamma*, the community of monastic disciples, assemble for meditation, chanting, praying, ordinations, recitations and rituals.

The congregational hall, *sim*

Viewed from afar, the most distinctive features of the *sim* are their multi-tiered roofs, cascading down in layers, the lowest flaring out, until they almost touch the ground. The style, although influenced by northern Thailand, is quintessentially Lao. The pillars supporting the roof and walls are sometimes made from entire tree trunks. The *sim* is a rectangle, and in some *wats* the walls lean outwards towards the roof line.

They were built of strong tropical wood, usually teak. Until the French arrived, there were no stone buildings in Laos, except in the far south at the Khmer ruins of Wat Phu. A few of the durable structures were brick and stucco, but most were wood from the surrounding tropical forests. As is the case for most artisans, the woodcarver's work was sacred, a task which would earn merit as well as providing visual pleasure. Instructions in classical texts categorised which woods were auspicious and how to propitiate the tree spirits before cutting the tree. Traditionally, further rites and ceremonies accompanied the creative process. The techniques of carving wood are several: icons are carved in the round from a block; decorative panels and door lintels are carved in high or low relief; incised carving, done freehand, is employed for flower and ornamental traceries.

The *sim* were elaborately carved, gilded, stencilled and

The veranaah of Wat Mai. Note the intricate decoration on the wall, columns, ceiling and beams.

frescoed, resulting in decoration of singular grace and harmony. "The ruling feature of Laotian decorative art is the rhythm of line and colour and the harmonious manner in which they combine to produce an agreeable visual sensation," writes Henri Marchal.

Originally real gold was used, panned from the Mekong river. Nowadays it is simply gold paint, although gold mining has started up again north of Luang Prabang. The use of real gold, as well as being lavish, is symbolic, as it is associated with the sun, the supreme light, and the gods. Gold would be lightly applied in thin layers, or laid on in the form of gold leaf. It could then be polished to a high gleam. Colour pigments were derived from natural sources including leaves such as indigo, tree bark, flowers and insects. Stucco was made with a mixture of limestone, sugar cane, buffalo skin, which boiled down makes glue, tree juice, bananas and water. Powdered limestone allows vapour to pass through and is well adapted to the tropical climate.

Wat Mai is where the Pra Bang was once housed. Officials would take an oath of allegiance in front of the holiest Buddha image in the town.

The use of stencils has its origins in China. At Dunhuang, in Western China, stencils made of paper and drawn in ink were found dating from the 8th century. The tradition may have made its way into Southeast Asia via trade routes and by the 17th century became widely practised in Luang Prabang temple decoration.

Gold stencilling is the most common way of decorating a temple. Wat Choum Kong (top) and Wat Sene (bottom).

Opposite: Dok so faa.
Wat Paphane (top),
Wat Nong (middle),
Wat Aham (middle right),
Wat Xieng Thong (bottom).

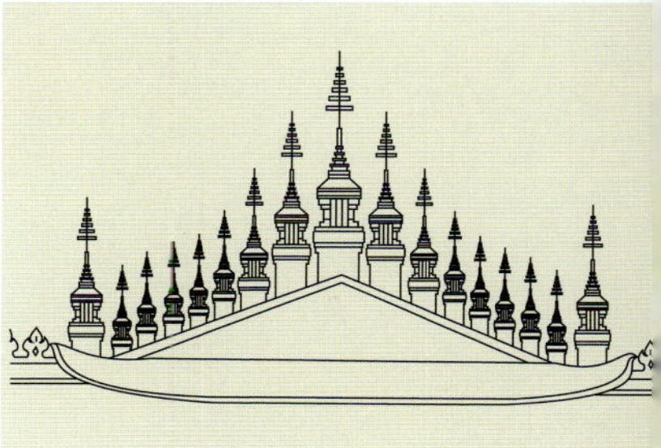

Metal roof decoration, *dok so faa*

On top of the tiled roof is a *dok so faa,* an elaborate metal decoration with great aesthetic appeal in the form of a row of parasols or miniature pagodas, or interlacing *nagas* pointing towards the heavens. They are symbols of the universe and of sacred Mount Meru. Tiered umbrellas are a symbol of royalty and a feature of both Hindu and Buddhist imagery of kings.

The roof finials, *cho faa*

The roofs end in more decoration, with ornate finials which point upwards towards the heavens, *cho faa,* literally sky cluster, adding a finishing upward sweep, creating an effect of lightness and balance. In some instances the roof edging is in the shape of a downward sloping *naga* with the head rearing upwards at the end. There are often crested projections in a row along the upper edge of the *naga's* body.

The verandah, *rabieng*

There is a verandah, *rabieng,* at the main entrance in front, and in larger *sim* at the back as well. It is a peristyle, with several columns, and the entrance portico is under the lowest of the superimposed tiered roofs.

The gable, *dok huang pheung*

The principal decorated space is the front gable and the winged gables at the side. The tympanum of the triangular gable is especially exquisitely carved, with details picked out in gold or colours, depicting deities or narrative scenes from the *Phra Lak Phra Lam,* or simply exuberant decorative motifs such as foliated scrolls. In some *wats* the main, eastern wall is stuccoed and then *bas reliefs,* two-dimensional carvings, are moulded and gilded.

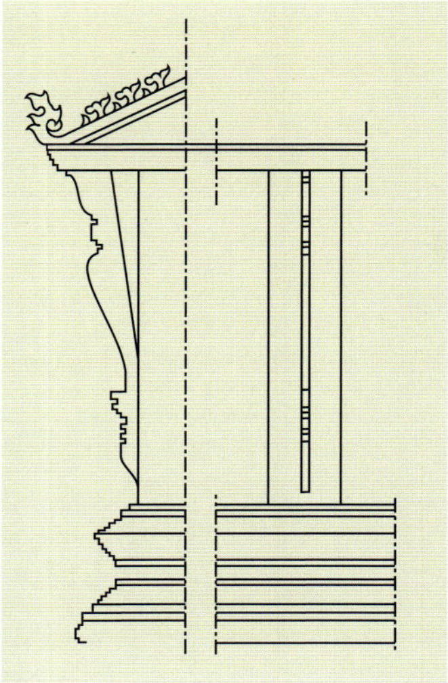

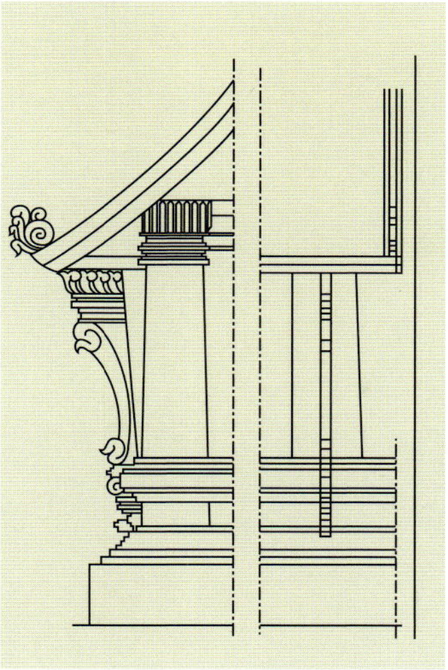

Beneath the gables, the doorways of the *wats* are always elaborately carved and exceptionally fine, depicting Rama and figures from the *Phra Lak Phra Lam* or mythical deities, surrounded by intertwined elements of the natural world such as foliage, floral and vegetal motifs as well as spirals, zoomorphic images and scenes from the Buddha's life. These doorways were praised by Henri Marchal: "It is within this framework that the beautiful door leaves of carved and gilded wood are set. In their wealth and sumptuousness they are probably the loveliest things to which Laotion art has given birth." The panels with their sacred images are a reminder that the temple is a residence for the divine presence and an earthly representation of the heavenly realm. Entering the *wat* is symbolic of moving from the terrestrial to the spiritual world, and the door symbolises the threshold. These doors are masterpieces, even in simple *wats*.

Top: *Drawings of eave brackets.*

Above left: *Wat Mai pediment.*

Above: *Drawing of door panels decoration of Wat Xieng Thong.*

Opposite top: Dok so faa, *Wat Xieng Thong.*

Opposite below: Naga *as eave brackets, Wat Mai.*

Top left: *The altar of the* sim, *Wat Mai.*

Above left: *Carved Buddhas in niches.*

Above: *Elaborately carved gable with scenes from the Life of the Buddha.*

Left: *Animals frequently occur in decoration.*

Opposite above: *Exterior stencil of Wat Xieng Thong.*

Opposite below: *Gold stencils on the interior black walls of Wat Xieng Thong.*

Inside the hallowed area of the *sim* the roof beams are almost always exposed, so that the structural system is visible, sometimes with a decorated tie-beam, the horizontal beam supporting the timbered roof, as well. The altar containing Buddha images is at the western end of the *sim,* facing the worshipper entering from the east. Everything is covered in religious iconography. The teak pillars are decorated with gold leaf and painted symbols. Dharma wheels, symbolising the Wheel of the Law, *dharmacakra,* are stencilled on to the beams. The ceiling might be covered with *dharma* wheels and bosses, projecting protuberances in the form of lotus buds or flowers. There are niches containing small Buddhas. Sometimes the walls are stencilled with narrative murals, ranging artistically from subtle finesse to hectic exuberance. These illustrate the *jataka* tales, the stories of the Buddha's previous lives (see Art and Religion p. 28).

Drawing of a devata *amidst elaborate foliate scrolls.*

As well as narratives, there are images of the *traiphum,* the 'three worlds' of Buddhist cosmology. Some are stencilled with gold leaf on to black or red walls. The mythical creatures depicted, include *kinaree,* half human and half bird, or *makaras,* aquatic demons consuming themselves, and serpents and extraordinary beasts, inspired by Khmer and Hindu mythology. Henri Marchal refers to the artistic exuberance of Laotian ornamentation, which "blends together fantastic beings and bodies whose anatomy is akin to foliation or to plants, heads strangely outlined, with fangs and threatening mouths, eyes with jagged-edged sockets; the quadrupeds have tails twisted in the form of scrolls and tipped with flames." He concludes that the complexity of these stencilled pictures creates the impression of a whirl of strange objects, glittering against the dark walls.

The stupa, *that*

Another important building in the *wat* compound is the *that.* This is a stupa or reliquary monument that historically enshrined relics of the Buddha himself, such as a hair or a piece of bone or of an important religious or royal personage. The shape originated in the Indian tradition of a burial mound that evolved into a bell shape with a graceful spire rising from the centre, a symbol of Mount Meru, crowned by a finial in the form of an umbrella or a lotus bud.

Gold stupa of Wat Xieng Thong.

Opposite: *Carved doors: Wat Visoun (top left), Wat Pa Khe (top right), Wat Visoun (bottom left), and window carved with guardian figures.*

Monks assembled in the sim.

The library, *hor tai*

One of the most significant buildings, only found in important *wats,* is the library or scripture repository. Its original function was the storage of illustrated, hand-written Buddhist scriptures, in Pali, on dried palm leaves bound together like a concertina. Most religious texts began as recited pieces, preserved in orally transmitted form, but gradually they came to be written down. The importance of these texts inspired scribes to produce manuscripts of considerable artistic merit.

To write on palm leaf, scribes incise the characters and drawings with a stylus on the outer face of the specially treated and cut leaves, then darken the cuts with turmeric and oil. Lacquered wooden covers protect the leaves which are hinged with cord and folded in accordion pleats. They are then wrapped in material and kept in special cabinets or boxes. By carefully storing them in a building raised above the ground on stilts the monks ensured that the damp of the tropical monsoon rains and insects, especially termites and white ants, would not destroy these treasures.

A monk studying palm leaf manuscripts.

The monks' quarters, *kutis*

The monks' quarters, *kutis,* are also important architecturally and historically, constructed in wood, carved and decorated, some with projecting verandahs, and blending harmoniously with the temple buildings. All of them have been protected under the World Heritage status.

The drum chapel, *hor kong*

This small, ornate building houses the important ceremonial drum, which possesses a *phi.* The drum is sounded daily for various prayers and festivities. With conservation and restoration work now under way, many of the temples look surprisingly new. Traditionally, they were always repainted annually after the rainy season, recalling the observations by Norman Lewis when he visited in the 1950s, "…everything is just a little too new, too spruce, too odorous of freshly applied varnish …. A year or two's neglect might greatly improve Luang Prabang."

Top: Kutis *in the grounds of Wat That Luang.*
Right: *A monk studying in Wat Xieng Thong.* (PP)

Location: Sakkarine Thanon (Road)
Date: 1559
Style: Luang Prabang Style II

*** Highlights**
Sweeping roofs
Tree of Life mosaic
Golden stencils on interior and exterior

Wat Xieng Thong

Situated at the tip of the promontory of Luang Prabang, where the Nam Khan river flows into the Mekong, the site is, so legend relates, where the first boundary stone of the city was laid to demarcate the territory of the city by two hermits who were brothers. They became its tutelary spirits. Wat Xieng Thong – *Xieng* meaning city and *Thong* meaning *bodhi* tree – was known as Temple of the Golden City and was considered a gateway to Luang Prabang. A steep, wide ceremonial staircase leading up from the river to the main entrance was for the kings who would sail downstream from the Royal Palace to visit Wat Xieng Thong. Other visiting dignitaries would also land at this port of embarkation when arriving from places such as Siam.

The most magnificent of all Lao *wats,* the finest example of sacred architecture in Laos, it was built by King Setthathirat, who ruled from 1548-1571. He built it in memory of the legendary King Chanthaphanith, whose stories are depicted inside the main *sim.* The temple survived numerous raids by Chinese marauders. It was this temple that persuaded UNESCO to make Luang Prabang a World Heritage Site.

Set in a peaceful compound, among ancient banyan trees, palms, frangipani and blazing scarlet and purple bougainvillea, this classical style *wat,* with all its shrines and chapels, radiates an aura of serenity. It is especially atmospheric in the late afternoon, as the sun drops behind the *wat.*

Opposite: *Façade of the* Sim *of Wat Xieng Thong.*

The sim, *with its sweeping low roofs, and the chapel of Wat Xieng Thong.*

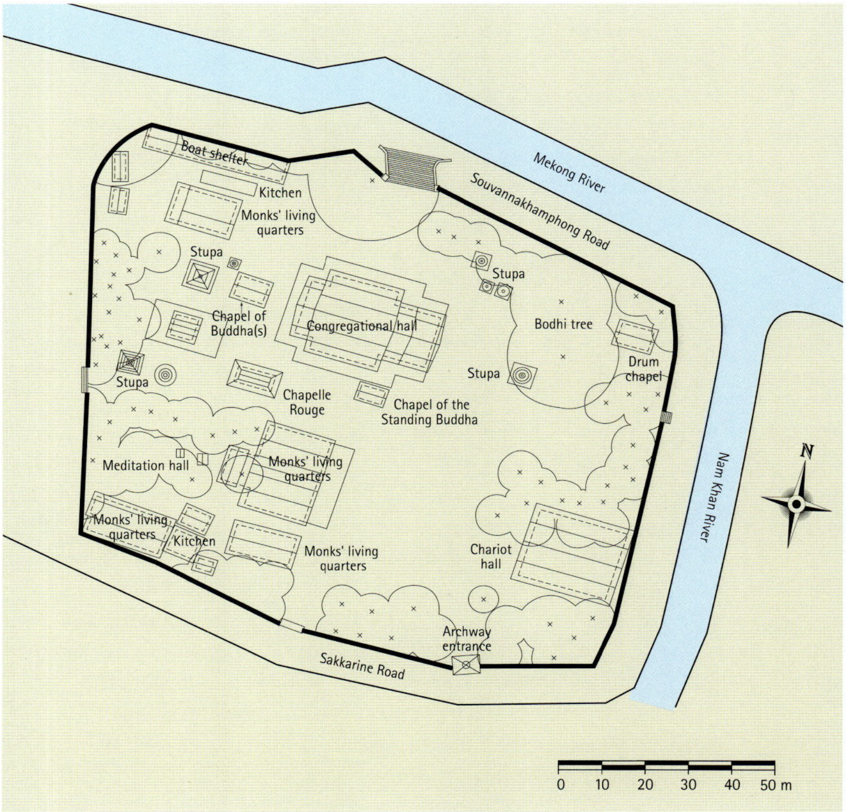
Mekong River
Souvannakhamphong Road
Nam Khan River
Sakkarine Road
Boat shelter
Kitchen
Monks' living quarters
Stupa
Chapel of Buddha(s)
Congregational hall
Stupa
Bodhi tree
Drum chapel
Stupa
Stupa
Chapelle Rouge
Chapel of the Standing Buddha
Meditation hall
Monks' living quarters
Monks' living quarters
Kitchen
Monks' living quarters
Chariot hall
Archway entrance
N
0 10 20 30 40 50 m

An old photo of the Gold stupa. (Courtesy University of Illinois)

Below: *A palanquin for a Buddha image used during the Lao New Year inside the assembly hall of Wat Xieng Thong. Note the* hanglin *at the top left of the picture.*

Central Area

The main *sim* was restored in 2012 and features the dramatic and distinctive Lao style of three successive red tiled roofs cascading down almost to the ground, and two-tiered lateral roofs, one at the western end and two at the eastern end over the main entrance, making a total of nine roofs. *Cho faa* rear up at the triangular tip of each roof, as if to raise them up again.

At first view, the roofs completely dominate the entire structure, like a huge elaborate crown with its golden *dok so faa.* As you approach, the gleaming gables and golden stencils start to become visible beneath the top heavy roof. The main portico has a gable supported by four black and gold rectangular columns, two tall and two shorter. Above the ornately carved golden gable with its double arcade is a tympanum, supported by the lotus petal capitals of the two main columns, between the two pointed tips of the roof. This is decorated with a rectangle containing two lavish golden *dharma* wheels in a red background, above which there is a square containing a third central *dharma* wheel. The edging of the roof is covered with golden motifs, while the inner underneath section is deep red and covered with more gold *dharma* wheels.

The external black painted walls of the main *sim* have a sumptuous jewel box appearance, covered from top to bottom with a riot of ornate gold stencils of deities and mythological animals. Golden carved eave brackets support the lowest roof which is edged with delicate golden pointed leaf-like forms. The quadruple rectangular openings of the wall are bordered by abstract golden motifs. Female deities on either side stand on top

An elephant's head on the side of the sim *is connected to the water channel inside the hall and delivers holy water to the lay people outside.* (PP)

of mythological lions with curling tails. Because of the lion's strength and majestic appearance it has always been associated with divinity and royalty in mythology. Deities are surrounded by images of the Buddha in meditation and small flying *apsaras* and divinities. At the top, flying *kinaree,* interspersed with small and large *dharma* wheels, fill almost every space in harmonious patterns.

On the north wall there is a tiny sculpted elephant's head, the god Ganesha, in silver mosaic. At Lao NewYear, *Pi Mai,* this head flows with holy water that comes from aspersions of the principle Buddha sculpture inside the *sim.* This is done with a *hanglin*, a long wooden *naga*. Water is poured into the tail and emerges from the mouth on to the image. People collect the water and take it home for prosperity in the coming year.

The back, western end, of the *sim* has a shimmering inlaid glass mosaic of a tree, the *Thong*, the *bodhi* tree, the Tree of Enlightenment, under which the Buddha meditated, after which the temple was named. Towards sunset, the details are picked out with sparkling clarity by the last rays of the sun. It was created by a local artist

The old photo of the chapel of the standing Buddha may be compared with that on page 67.
(Courtesy University of Illinois)

The tree of life at the back of the sim *is the highlight of this temple.*

Thao Sing Kèo in 1960, at the same time as the mosaics in one of the chapels in the compound, the chapels in the compound, the *chapelle rouge,* and those in the throne room of the Royal Palace, commissioned by Savang Vatthana. Its imagery, the tree of life motif, recurs throughout Southeast Asia and is a cosmological symbol of the *axis mundi;* the link between the heavens, the earth and the underworld. Trees are also resonant with notions of cosmic unity, as their roots reach down into the ground and their branches stretch upwards to heaven. Other legends surrounding the symbolism of the tree here include that of two hermits who demarcated the territory of the future city near the tree of life. This mosaic, flanked by two round columns covered in black and gold, depicts, in a charming naïve style, the tree in the centre with thick branches. At the foot of the tree there is a seated tiger, as well as prancing deer, a cow with her calf lying on the ground, fluttering birds and a pilgrim walking with his stick. These are said to be representations from Lao fables. Above, on the lower branches, are two magnificent peacocks, of symbolic importance in Hinduism. In the *Rig Veda,* the sacred Hindu texts dating from 1200 BC, the steeds of Indra, god of thunder, rain and war, were said to have hair like the feathers of a peacock. The *Ramayana* also alludes to the transformation of the gods into animal form to escape the wicked Ravana. Indra became a peacock. The peacock destroys snakes and the suggestive eye motifs of its lustrous feathers are said to have been a thousand eyes, enabling it to do so. It was believed that they swallowed the snake's venom, using it to create its colourful plumage. The Hindu god Skanda was depicted riding a snake-killing peacock. Skanda used poisons to create a magical elixir of immortality. Above the peacocks other birds perch on the successive branches, bedecked with pretty leaves. At the top of the tree are *kinaree,* and above stands a golden Buddha, his arms by his side, with a purple, mauve and gold stupa rising up behind, and supplicants on their knees on either side of him. Doorways on either side of the tree mosaic are carved with golden images of Rama, as are the other doors leading into the *sim.*

At the main, eastern entrance, the white steps up to the *sim* have newel posts in the form of lotus buds, covered with turquoise mosaic. As if the visitor were not sufficiently bedazzled by the exterior, the interior,

Wat Xieng Thong mosaic tiger.

Wat Xieng Thong Gong.

Wat Xieng Thong Apsara on door.

although dark and lit only with candles and dim lightbulbs, is filled with more golden images. Supported by cylindrical and rectanglar columns, the ceiling and walls are covered with a wealth of stencilling. These would have been created originally with real gold leaf, and although nowadays it is only gold paint, they still glow in the subdued light. The ceiling is decorated with black squares containing gold *dharma* wheels, the corners of the square enhanced by lotus motifs that project like the bosses of medieval cathedrals. Floral, vegetal and geometric patterns provide a background for numerous anthropomorphic and zoomorphic figures, some half beast, half man, others half bird, half man, *kinaree*. Myths and legends such as the tales of King Chanthaphanith, a simple betel nut merchant who supposedly came to do business in Laos and eventually became the king, are shown.

There are also depictions of the *Traiphum*. The heavens feature little palaces in which the Buddha sits crosslegged in the meditation pose, while celestial deities appear overhead, and Rama appears in a fine horse-drawn chariot, protected by a parasol. The earth has delicate golden trees, including minutely detailed palm trees, dotting the landscape in which people walk or kneel, singly or in pairs. The hells depict people being punished in horrible ways such as crucifixion, burning in cauldrons of boiling liquid, being cut up or hanged or whipped, but they are all drawn with the utmost delicacy. These images are, of course, didactic and intended to warn pilgrims of the wages of sin.

Green mosaic lotus buds on top of the newel posts.

Gold stencilling on the interior walls.
Above: *Part of the* traiphum *depicting hell.*

Opposite: *The tale of King Chanthaphanith, a legendary character of Luang Prabang.*

The soon-to-be Buddha seated in meditation under the Bodhi tree, tempted by the demon Mara, with his army who point lotus-tipped arrows at Siddharta Gautama. As Gautama touches the earth in bhumisparsa mudra, *the earth goddess below, Nang Thorani, standing in a* tribangha *pose, wrings out the water from her hair that will drown the army.*

A jataka *tale.*

Detail showing a kinaree.

Stencilling on the interior wall of a jataka *tale. Note the flat perspective, the random order of the narrative, and the categorisation of the figures, in which lay people wear sarongs and plain tops and heavenly figures wear elaborate costumes. Note also the three* nagas *at the bottom of the picture.*

Right and opposite: *The principal Buddha image of Wat Xieng Thong is surrounded by numerous smaller images. Placing many statues on or near the altar is a common practice in Luang Prabang temples. There are more standing Buddha sculptures in the corridor. When new statues come in, the old ones are removed to a side chapel.* (Opposite, PP)

The pediment of the Chapel of the Standing Buddha is elaborately carved, gilded and encrusted with glass mosaic.

Below: *Stupas in the compound. The one on the right is octagonal with the animals of the cardinal points on each side.* (PP)

Outside, the rest of the compound has four other significant chapels and several gilded stupas of different designs. Two of the chapels are alongside the south wall of the main *sim,* one of which is the Chapel of the Standing Buddha. Its pediment is richly decorated with an inlay of coloured glass, with a lotus in the centre. Two small figures of *kinaree* stand on either side at the base of the pediment.

The front of the Chapel of the Standing Buddha beside the sim. *Inside is a Buddha image in the* abhayamudra *pose.* (OC)

Next to the Chapel of the Standing Buddha is the charming small red chapel, often referred to as *La Chapelle Rouge,* from the period of French scholarship. This houses a reclining Buddha, its robe curling outwards at the feet, the hands supporting the head. It was taken to Paris for the great exhibition in 1931, and then returned to Vientiane where it stayed until 1964 before being brought back and reinstated in the chapel. The exterior has a mosaic, created in the 1950s to celebrate the Buddha's *nirvana* of 2,500 years ago, on a pink background with images in vividly coloured glass. These recall the mosaics in the Throne Room of the Royal Palace and are in a similar style. Even though the colours are bright, they are extraordinarily delicate and have an engaging naïve quality. The heavens are shown in the upper register, with seated Buddhas in shrines, while below is the terrestrial world, with houses on stilts, chickens and animals, and people running, playing football, and going about their daily lives among trees and flowers.

Below and above left:
La Chapelle Rouge.

The Buddha lay down after his ultimate meditation and entered mahaparanirvana, *passing from the terrestrial to the celestial realm. Note the robe,* antaravasaka, *curling outwards at the feet as if the Buddha were standing, a stylistic device typical of Lao imagery.*

Below: *The library or* hor tai, *housing Buddhist manuscripts. One of Luang Prabang's most revered Buddha images, Pra Maan, resides here. The locals pray to him if they wish to have children.*

Above: *The Chariot hall. Both the building and the chariot are the work of Pae Ton.*

Left: *Wat Xieng Thong Funerary Chapel Ramayana Carving.*

Opposite: *Details of the glass mosaic decoration on the walls of the Chapelle Rouge depicting scenes from everyday life.* (PP)

Wat Xieng Thong Funerary Chapel Marica.

The Chapel of the Funeral Chariot, *hor latsalot,* contains the hearse of King Sisavangvong, father of the last sovereign, Savang Vatthana, who ordered the building of this chapel. Sisavangvong was crowned in 1946 and died in 1959. His ashes are in a stupa in Wat That Luang. The chapel contains his funeral chariot and cremation urn. At times, the old *Ramayana* puppets, the *tookatahs,* that belonged to the royal family, are displayed in glass cases along the north wall.

The small drum chapel, with its gilded, carved gable, contains the gongs which are sounded daily at 4pm during particular lunar periods and at festivals.

Ceremonial rowing boats are kept in special sheds in temple compounds for religious festivals associated with water and the seasons.

With its wealth of images from the *Phra Lak Phra Lam* on all the door and window panels, this chapel shows that even in the 1950s and 60s highly skilled artists and wood carvers were working in Luang Prabang. The entire narrative was designed by Manivong Khattiyarat (also known as Manivong Khattignarath) who was Director of the Royal Ballet. His method was to sketch the imagery directly on to the wood panels and was designed to be read in a counter-clockwise direction. His team worked under the supervision of his teacher Phia Sing (1898-1967), who was a master of ceremonies to the kings and a celebrated royal chef. The late Alan Davidson, British Ambassador to Laos in the 1970s, described Phia Sing as 'physician, architect, choreographer, sculptor, painter and poet'. Also involved were master woodcarver Phia Thit Tanh (1909-2000) and Thit Bounthan, who made the glass mosaics for the structure. It was created between 1973-1975.

Above the main doors an intricately carved panel depicts the leading characters from the epic. The two main doors that open inwards show on the left side an alluring image of *Nang Sida* (Sita), bejewelled and bare-breasted, with one hand stroking the golden deer Marica that she has spotted in the forest and wants to possess. The right hand door panel shows her coquettishly posed with *Phra Ram* (Prince Rama), with one hand raised, persuading him to capture the deer that will prove their downfall, while he envelops her tenderly in his arms, looking down on Marica with a sad, almost prescient expression.

Wat Xieng Thong Funerary Urn.

On the right hand side of these doors is a striking carving of Nang Sida when she had to prove to Phra Ram, by an ordeal of fire, that she had been faithful to him while imprisoned by *Totsakan* (Ravana). Sida's many instances of suffering in the epic are poignant, yet her unfailing innocence and virtue ensure that she passes through this harrowing test unscathed. Her hands are joined in prayer as the flames, in glittering gold, appear to engulf her, giving her the air of a martyr.

Inside the chapel, the king's funerary urn, in intricately carved and gilded wood, resembles a jar in which the deceased monarch would have been placed in foetal position prior to his cremation. Two other smaller urns contained the remains of his parents. There are many gilded wooden Buddhas at the back, in the *hiek fone mudra* standing against walls of more glass mosaics.

Gilded wooden Buddhas standing against glass mosaic wall.

Location: Confluence Nam Khan and Mekong rivers.
Date: 1773 (dates vary)
Style: Luang Prabang Style I

*** Highlights**
Graceful door panels

WAT PAK KHAN

The name derives from its location at the tributary of the Nam Khan and Mekong. Built by Phagna Chanthep under King Inta Som (r. 1727-76), it was reconstructed in the early 20th century.

The *sim* has a two-tiered tiled roof, independent of each other, and four windows on either side with simply carved wooden eave brackets in the form of *nagas*. The eastern entrance has a main door with two smaller doors on either side.

This old, simple and peaceful *wat*, has just been restored. In particular the attractively carved door panels and window shutters have been carefully renovated and in their pristine state are a perfect example of the gentle, understated sacred art of Luang Prabang.

Notice in particular the two elegantly depicted images of Rama on the central panels of the main doorway. Each has a serene smile and radiant expression, with a tall pointed crown and a halo and two sets of arms, revealing his divine status, with an elaborate close-fitting regal costume, poised like a slender dancer with long legs in graceful movements and delicate hand gestures, above an image of Hanuman, who is on bended knee, with similarly dancerly grace.

The two smaller doors on either side feature carvings of spiralling circular tendrils of foliage, each tendril culminating in a small divinity emerging from the tip of the branch, with hands joined in prayer.

Villagers tend to enter via a door on the northern side, as it is closer to the road, whereas the monks usually use the door on the southern side, closest to their living quarters.

Wat Pak Khan Rama Face.

Wat Pak Khan.

An old photo of Wat Pak Khan. Note the Xieng Kouang roof style.
(Courtesy University of Illinois)

Assembly hall of the temple. Note the height of the roof line above the ground.

The temple at present which has not changed much compared to the old photo opposite.

Door panels with motifs from the Ramayana *epic.*

Location: Sakkarine Road, opposite Wat Xieng Thong
Date: 1773
Style: Luang Prabang Style II

*** Highlight**
Glass mosaics on *sim*

Opposite: *An old photo of Wat Khili.*
(Courtesy University of Illinois)

The sim *of Wat Khili with its gold columns and red paint.*

Wat Khili (Wat Souvanna Khili)

Temple of the Golden Mountain, built during the 18th century by Chao Kham Sattha, who came from the northern Xieng Kouang province and built his temple in a style reminiscent of those found in the mountains close to the Plain of Jars. The building of the *wat* reinstated the relationship between Xieng Kouang and Luang Prabang.

The collection of buildings form an unusual blend of French colonial and Lao temple architecture.

The *sim* has one pair of dark gold columns at the main entrance. A rear hall and stupa at the back are characteristics of this style, with a double roof. It has a single nave and porch. The outer walls are decorated with fine glass mosaics of trees, three on either side of the entrance. The roof finials of *nagas* are complemented by abstract shaped *cho faa* all along the end of the gable to the uppermost tip of the roof. The window shutters are carved with gilded images showing two people on one panel, and a figure, possibly Prince Siddharta Gautama, on the other panel. Above them zoomorphic figures decorate the walls. A deep, ornately carved gable, with two concave arches, completes the elaborate decorative scheme. The chamber housing the main Buddha image is at the back of the *sim.*

Top: *Wat Khili monk's living quarter. Note the colonial style of the building.*

Left: *Detail of the tree of life glass mosaic on the wall of the* sim.

On the road side of the compound is a white two storey building which houses the monks. Built of brick and white stucco, with its square windows with gracious curved tops and first floor projecting verandah, it looks more like a French villa, crowned with a two tiered temple roof with Lao motifs.

One of the small buildings within the *wat* compound houses a permanent exhibition of historic black and white photographs of monks dating back to the 1890s from the Buddhist Archive of Luang Prabang. This collection was established by the venerated late Abbot of Wat Sene, Phra Khamchan Virachitta Maha Thera. It was discovered and studied by photographer Hans Georg Berger.

Opposite: *Window panels of the* sim *showing perhaps the* Vessantara Jataka.

Location: Sakkarine Road, close to Wat Xieng Thong.
Date: 1758
Style: Luang Prabang Style II

*** Highlight**
Gable with *dharma* wheels

Wat Si Boun Houang

Historians claim it was built in the reign of King Sotika Kuman (1776-81) although its origins are earlier.

A modest, quiet *wat* with a smaller *sim,* with an elevated base reached by plain white steps. Restored in the early 1900s, it originally had gold stencilled painting on the lateral walls and porch. Four columns, of which two are square and two round, with lotus petal capitals, are decorated in gold and red abstract designs. They support a gable with images of *dharma* wheels. The main façade is white with a richly decorated golden doorway, the stucco lintel and pediments rising up in successive layers. The two tiered roof is edged along its entire length with delicate *cho faa.* Palm trees and frangipani give shade in the courtyard.

The temple at present. Note the Xieng Khouang roof style that sweeps down low.

Wat Si Boun Houang in the past.
(Courtesy University of Illinois)

Monks robing at Wat Si Boun Houang.

Location: Kuonxoa Road
Date: 18th century
Style: Luang Prabang Style II

*** Highlight**
Elaborate *cho faa* finials

Wat Siri Moung Khoung

The *sim* of this *wat* is simple and whitewashed with an attached verandah along the north wall. But in spite of its modest appearance it has an exuberant two-tiered roof with elaborate *cho faa* finials and elegant carved eave brackets. Four plain undecorated cylindrical columns support a gable with abstract gold designs. There is one portico on the main entrance, and three small windows with five eave brackets on the southern wall. *Cho faa* decorate both lengths of the pitched roof in front. Two stucco white lions with large, ferocious grins stand guard. A small white chapel is located by the side of the southern wall, and there are large succulents and cacti growing in the compound.

The assembly hall. Note that the exterior peristyle only runs down one side.

Location: Kounxoa Road.
Date: originally 1500s
Style: Luang Prabang Style III

*** Highlight**
Gable with gold foliate designs.

Wat Sop

According to legend, it was built by King Theng Kham (r. 1479-86), the son of King Sao Takaphat Phene Phao (r. 1438-79), to commemorate the king's death in a battle near Lane Xang in 1479. It was restored in 1909.

The *sim* has a three tiered roof. The gable features gold foliate images in a geometrical harmony with five levels. There are five rectangular columns on either side, with four cylindrical columns on the main verandah with gold lotus petal capitals. The gable is decorated in gold foliate and vegetal designs. There is just one portico. The two windows in the south and north walls are noteworthy for their Khmer style carved wooden balusters. The two peristyles were added in 1950.

An old photo of the temple before the assembly hall had a side peristyle.
(Courtesy University of Illinois)

The assembly hall with short pillars supporting the later peristyle roof.

Top: *Foliate design of the assembly hall's gable.*

Location: Sakkarine Road.
Date: 1718
Style: Luang Prabang Style II

*** Highlight**
Stencils of deities and mythical animals on exterior walls

WAT SENE (WAT SENSOUKARAM)

Built in 1714, by Tia Tiao, during the reign of King Kithsarat (r. 1707-25), Wat Sene is the Temple of the Patriarch. Restoration work was carried out in the 1930s, and again in 1957, to celebrate the 2,500 years since the birth of the historical Buddha.

Located prominently on the main road, the bright terracotta colour of this temple and its main *sim* with its four-tiered roof is offset by brilliant gold decoration applied straight on to the walls. It lacks the subtlety of other temples, being newly repainted in vivid primary colours. More Thai in style, the *sim* of yellow and red was originally built in 1714, but later restored. Ornate windows contain four carved balusters with pictures of deities behind them on the panels, and a delicate triangular gold painted pattern stencilled at the top. The main door is crowned by a rising high relief pediment formed like a stupa and culminating in a golden spire. Created in 1960, it features stencils on either side of the doorway of *apsaras* resembling in style those of Angkor Wat in Cambodia.

On either side of each window there appear single slender deities wearing pointed crowns and holding lotus blossoms, some standing on mythical horses, others on lions. A unicorn is depicted, a beast that appears in many ancient myths all over the world and is a symbol of chastity. A single-horned beast symbolised the power of kings and gods, a sign of virility. The doorways have similar triangular decorations and deities posed on mythical lions, and the balance of the figures in relation to the window and doorway is one of rhythm and harmony. Doors have carved gilded figures of more divinities and mythical animals.The columns are square rather than rounded.

To the left of the monk's assembly hall in the middle of the picture, is the lay people's assembly hall. Note the drum chapel on the far right.

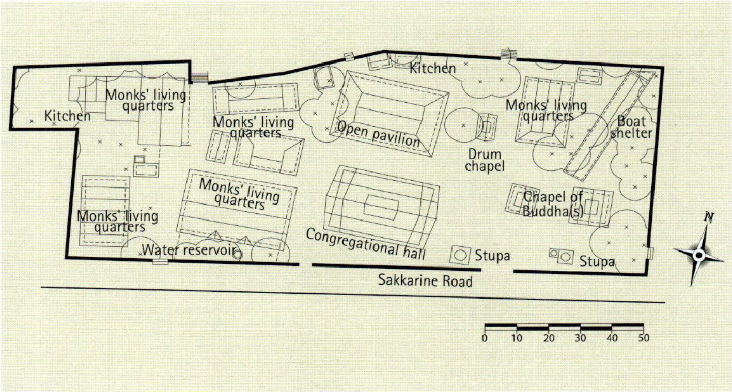

Old photo of Wat Sene.
(Courtesy University of Illinois)

Below left: *Window with graceful balusters and gold stencilling.*

Below: *Door panels of monk's assembly hall.*

The interior is similarly decorated with golden stencils of deities and animals on a red background. A side chapel houses a large standing Buddha statue with a drum. The golden gable, made in 1960 of gilded cement, features three registers with, at the top, the Buddha on Mount Meru. In the lower register the Buddha descends a glittering staircase accompanied by Brahma and Indra. In the lowest register he is preaching to a community.

Left: *Interior of the* sim *depicting heavenly figures, mythical animals and Luang Prabang Style II's roof style.*

Above: *The stair leading up to the lay people's* sim.

Below: *Detail of the foliate garland on the door panels.*

The sim *in which lay people listen to sermons and participate in Buddhist ceremonies.*

Above and below: *Chapel housing a large standing Buddha image, which was removed from Wat That Noi when it was demolished.*

Drawing of the sim *door.*

Location: Kounxoa Road
Date: 1729
Style: Luang Prabang III

*** Highlight**
Bronze Buddha statue imbued with miraculous powers

Wat Nong Sikhunmuang

This temple was built in 1729 during the reign of King Inta Som (1727-76). In 1774 when fire raged in the town, it burned down, but a bronze statue was spared. It was restored in 1804 and renamed Wat Nong.

Extensively restored now by the Thais, set on a reinforced concrete base, the *sim,* with a single nave and porch, is very bright and polished looking. It is in a simple style with a vivid orange tiled three-tiered roof and gleaming golden *dok so faa* with seven parasols on either side of the central one, suggesting that this was built for a king. The entrance has six square columns and a carved gable with abstract swirling patterns of gold on red. Side staircases have glistening silver *nagas.* It has five windows and a door on each side, as well as the main portico. During various festivals it is even more colourful with children and young novice monks in bright orange.

Inside there is a much venerated bronze Buddha statue, Pra Chao Ong Saensaksid, which, according to oral tradition was brought by a merchant from Ban Koom Sayla village, north of Luang Prabang. After trading in Chiang Saen, he had intended to transport the Buddha back home. However, his raft stopped close to this temple, and he decided to install it here. During a fire in 1774, the statue miraculously survived. Since then local people come to pray here prior to embarking on a journey.

Left and opposite top: *Wat Nong Sikhunmuang during a festival.*

Opposite: *An old photo of Wat Nong Sikhunmuang.*
(Courtesy University of Illinois).

Location: Sakkarine Road on the corner of Savang Vatthana Road.
Date: 1645, according to Parmentier, but 1815 according to Chao Khaminanh Vongkot Rattana, historian of Luang Prabang.
Style: Luang Prabang Style III

*** Highlight**
Central doorway with golden architrave and pediment

WAT PA PHAI

Known as the Monastery of the Bamboo Forest, its construction date is disputed.

This ornately decorated but simple style single-nave temple has a classic Lao-Thai mural over the gilded and carved wooden façade. It shows scenes of everyday life in Laos. The exuberant doorway has two sets of ornate columns, the first black and the second set red, with gilded stencil decorations. The architrave around the main doorway rises in triplicate, the three successive pediments terminating with birds, resembling cockerels, in profile, whose tails furl in the form of scroll-shaped volutes. The tympanum shows two more extravagant looking birds, probably peacocks, in gold. The door panels display Rama, in a dance-like leaping position, holding a long staff, one foot on top of a lion whose tail curls around. There is a single nave.

An old photo of Wat Pa Phai. (Courtesy University of Illinois)

Opposite: *Shrine in temple compound.*

Murals on the façade of the sim *show scenes from everyday life.*

The door to the sim *has very detailed carved and gilded decoration embellished with glass mosaic.* (PP)

Opposite top: *The pediment above the* sim *doorway. Note the protruding peacock in the centre.*

Opposite below: *The front verandah.*

Location: Sotika Kuman Road.
Date: *sim* dates back to 1879
Style: Luang Prabang Style II

*** Highlight**
School for stencilling and laquerwork

Wat Sieng Mouan (Xieng Mouan)

Originally built in 1853 by Phragna Sisonxay, during the reign of King Chantarath (1851-72), it was known at first as the Monastery of Melodious Sounds, Wat Sieng Mouan, owing to the harmony of its drums, and then as the Monastery of the Joyous Town.

This *wat* features a two-tiered roof, with a single porch and triple nave. There are six doors and three windows. When it was restored in 1964, more windows were added. Above the doorway the lintel and pediment are richly carved and gilded with closely intertwining floral motifs symmetrically balanced. On either side brilliantly coloured murals depict the life of the Buddha, including, on the top right, teaching his acolytes and mid-right, passing into *mahaparanirvana*. Note the four roundels in the carved gable with Buddha images.

The *wat* also has a school in a building in the compound specialising in teaching novice monks traditional arts and crafts. These include lacquer work, stencilling, painting, glass mosaic, wood carving, sculpture and other temple decoration. Part of the training focuses on repairs and the preparation of traditional mortar. Started by UNESCO, the project has been funded by a grant from Norway. There is a small exhibition room which shows some of their work and photographs of previous achievements.

Left: *The central entrance to the assembly hall.*

Right: *Inside the assembly hall.*

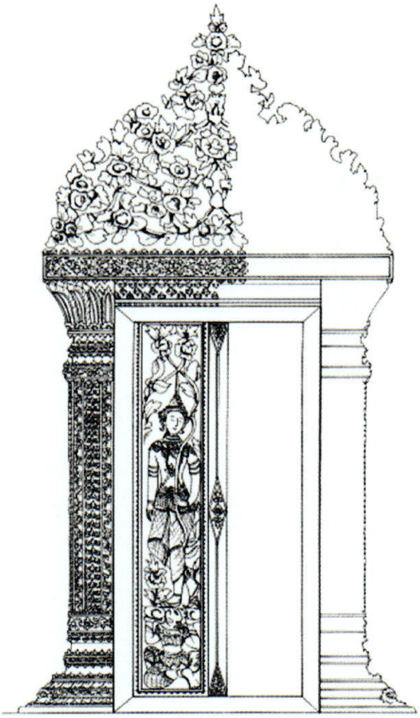

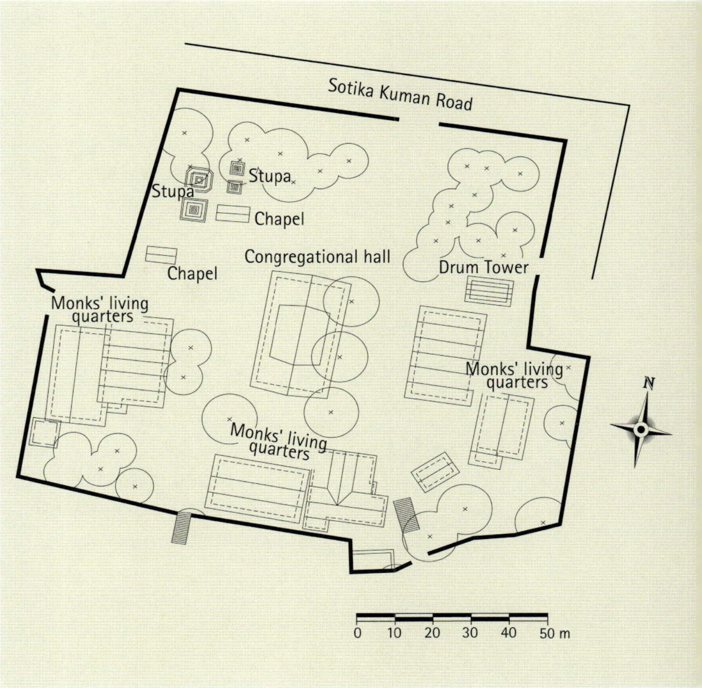

A drawing of the doorway.

An old photo of Wat Sieng Mouan.
(Courtesy University of Illinois)

The assembly hall.

Location: Sotika Kuman Road.
Date: Completed 1855
Style: Luang Prabang Style II

Wat Choum Khong

A 19th century temple with two Chinese gods guarding the entrance, is near Wat Sieng Mouan. It has four columns and in addition to the main portico has five other entrances. It has been renovated and painted brilliant white. The columns are gold on black and the young monks have restored all the stencilled images, including the recessed panels above the doorway. The main portico has a superimposed lintel heavily gilded and decorated. The supporting eave brackets are of a curvilinear design. The windows are deeply recessed with new stencilling of gold on black.

Wat Choum Khong was started in 1843 under King Sukaseum (r. 1836-51) by the Venerable Keo. Adhering to the classic style, it has a triple nave with four bays, seven windows and a single porch with three doors. Its name refers to a Buddha statue cast, it is said, from a bronze gong. It has been restored three times in 1933, 1951 and 1963.

A drawing of sim *door panels.*

An old photo of Wat Choum Khong. (Courtesy University of Illinois)

Opposite: *Wat Choum Khong during restoration by monks.*

Location: Phousi Road
Date: 1799
Style: Luang Prabang Style II

*** Highlight**
Splendid columns

Wat Paphane (Wat Pafang)

The Monastery of the Flame Tree Forest, is in the same compound alongside Wat Pha Khe. It was originally constructed by Sene Mu Xa, a wealthy man, during the reign of King Anourat (1791-1817).

It has a three-tiered roof, and whitewashed walls with a verandah with four cylindrical red and gold columns, two short and two long, whose capitals resemble those of classical Corinthian columns. Their red and gold decoration is very faded, as is the portico and gable. Otherwise there is very little decoration on this rather deserted looking *wat.* There are three windows on either side, the north and south.

An old photo of Wat Paphane.
(Courtesy University of Illinois)

The somewhat neglected sim *today.*

WAT PA KHE (WAT SIPHOUTTABATH)

Location: Phousi Road
Date: Reconstructed in 1851
Style: Thai style

*** Highlight**
Dutch doors

The Monastery of the Forest of Khe Trees – *Sesbania grandiflora leguminosae* – was built during the reign of King Chantarath (1851-72). Its main attractions are the enchanting carved doors showing a Dutch merchant, possibly based on one of the first Europeans to visit Laos, Gerrit van Wuysthoff, from Holland, who came to Laos in 1641-42. But, according to some sources, it is more likely that the artist was inspired by Chinese prints, as the monastery was built by King Chantarath in honour of a mission of special envoys from Luang Prabang to Kunming in China, under the then emperor Ton Zhi. At that time Luang Prabang sought to counterbalance the enveloping power of Siam.

Situated close to Mount Phousi, and alongside Wat Paphane, this is an attractive but rather faded temple.

It has a three tiered roof and four hexagonal pillars, with a tympanum and façade edging containing inlaid mosaics. One of its three sets of red wooden doors shows two images of Rama in the form of Dutch merchants. Note the costume of each, as the figure, with his gentle half smile, wears a jaunty tricorn hat with two feathers and ribbons, long hair, and a finely made close-fitting jacket, with pleats at the bottom, and a belt looped over. He wears a pleated skirt, offset by long embossed boots with thick soles, and carries a crop in each hand. On each shoulder is a parrot. Below his feet is an animal with long ears resembling a baby water buffalo looking up at him. The background shows finely detailed palm trees and leaves. The harmony and flowing lines, detail and subtle wit, make these very fine examples of Lao art and intriguing historically.

Side view of the sim.

An old photograph of the facade of the sim.
(Courtesy University of Illinois)

Window panels.

Door panels depicting the Dutch merchant.

Door panels with figures from Phra Lak Phra Lam.

Wat Pa Khe Dutch Merchant Face.

The other set of doors show more traditional guardian figures, delicately carved, blowing conches. One is standing on a deer, the other on a tiger.

The window shutters on the south side also contain images of a foreign merchant, with a loose fitting shirt depicted in folds, and a loose belt tied in a knot around his waist, and pointed shoes. His hair is shown in strands, and like the Dutch figure on the front, he has a bird on either shoulder. On the right shoulder it is a parrot. Below his feet is a dog, symbol of fidelity, rather than the mythical beasts depicted on so many Lao door panels.

Note the swastika signs on the low walls in front of the main door, reminiscent of those at Wat Phra Mahathat. In Sanskrit *svasti,* is symbolic of the energy of the sun, and the arms of the swastika point in the cardinal directions. When the sign is shown with the arms pointing clockwise, it represents the creative energy of the sun. The anti-clockwise swastika refers to winter sun and is not auspicious.

The interior has murals, described by Henri Parmentier as ridiculous and crude. Showing Chinese influence, they depict a Lao delegation in China, paying homage to Ton Zhi, the emperor. There are others showing scenes from the *Phra Lak Phra Lam.*

The assembly hall.

Location: Close to the 328 steps to Wat Phousi.
Date: 1861
Style: Thai Style

*** Highlight**
Chinese style murals

WAT PA HUAK

This small 19th century *wat* is close to the 328 steps up to Wat Phousi, opposite the Royal Palace.

It has a two-tiered roof and a carved wooden gable that is rather faded and weathered but is undergoing renovation. The gable has a carved *garuda,* half-bird, half-man, a *naga* and Indra on his mount, the elephant Erawan. The upright profile of the building and *cho faa* of the roof are in the form of a *naga,* similar to Thai *wats*. Other details of the ornamentation also show Siamese and Cambodian influence. There are inlaid mosaics on the façade. Close by are the steps to Wat Phousi, set amid perfumed frangipani trees, which make the walk up such a pleasure. The white and yellow fragrant petals often litter the ground around the *wat* and steps.

This Monastery of the Bamboo Forest, was built in 1861 in honour of the forest, during the reign of King Chantarath (1851-72), by a nobleman, Phra Sri Mahanam, who was acquainted with the Thai royal family during the reign of King Rama V.

There are two murals on the upper right hand wall depicting deities with crowns and halos weaving for the royal court. The looms of traditional Lao design are painted with great detail and accuracy, showing the warp and weft, shuttle and sword and a section of woven silk. The feet of one of the deities on the bamboo foot treadle are especially delightful with red coloured toes of equal length.

Three Buddha images in bhumisparca mudra, *with murals behind them.*

The back of Wat Pa Huak viewed from street level.

The interior has murals which, instead of showing stories of the Buddha, depict the legend of Jambupati-Suta, a king said to have magical powers but an aggressive character. He held sway over a smaller kingdom ruled by King Phimphisan, and the latter complained to the Lord Buddha. The Lord Buddha called Jambupati-Suta to persuade him to behave more gently, but he resisted. Finally a battle ensued, which was won by the Buddha. The murals show a final panel with a congregation of monks, and the ordained Jambupati-Suta taking his place among them. Painted by two artists, one of whom may have studied painting in Bangkok, and another who may have come from southern China, the pictures are in a Chinese style. King Phimphisan appears as a Chinese dignitary, in a city that looks Chinese. There are scenes of daily life, capturing, in particular, images of Chinese people who settled in Luang Prabang.

The strange juxtaposition of styles was condemned by Henri Parmentier – perhaps unfairly – as "ridiculous, but less awful than those at Wat Pa Khe." Because of the Thai connections, the murals were restored during the 1990s with the help of the city of Chiang Mai and the Faculty of Fine Arts at the University of Chiang Mai which co-operated and helped teach skills to Lao restorers.

Wat Pa Huak in the midst of trees seems to have changed little over the years.

Location Mount Phousi
Date: (unknown)
Style: shrine

*** Highlight**
Wooded location with good view

Wat Tham Phousi

This small open-sided *wat,* almost like a wayside shrine, is literally built up against the rock. It has a two-tiered roof ending in *cho faa* and supported by two hexagonal columns with lotus petal capitals at the top, decorated in red and gold. There is a simple carved gable of red and gold with a Buddha at the centre of swirling foliage and floral decorative motifs. There is a large Buddha image within, wide of girth, in the style known as *Pha Kachai.* The foundation with steps up to the *wat* has rustic painted murals featuring a sylvan scene of trees and mountains.

Opposite: *Buddha images inside Wat Tham Phousi.* (OC)

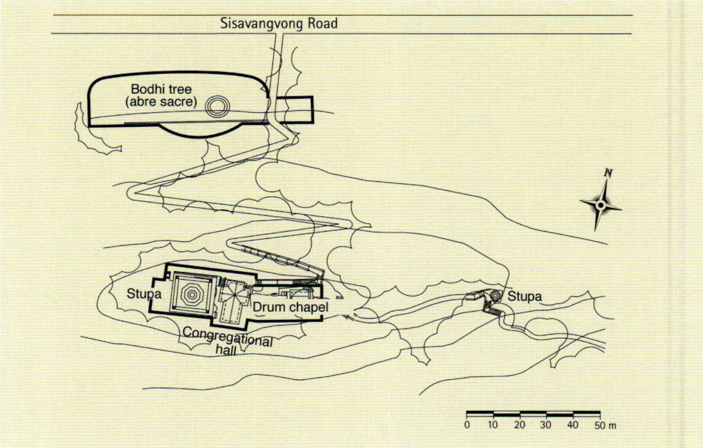

Wat Tham Phousi and the rock upon which it is built.
(Courtesy University of Illinois)

Location: On top of Mount Phousi, the centre of the town, opposite the Royal Palace.
Date: 1804
Style: Classical Lao

* **Highlights**
Golden dome and great view

That Chomsi

The 328 steps leading up through frangipani trees are delightful if quite demanding, but you can stop halfway up and admire the view. *Phou Si* means sacred hill; That Chomsi is the small *wat* at the top. Built in 1804, its golden stupa, in classical Lao form on a rectangular base, shimmers in the sun making it visible from afar. It is being restored and has murals. There are spectacular views of the surrounding mountains and river, and it is especially dramatic at sunset as the last rays slip behind the silhouetted mountains. Everyone comes up here for the incomparable view, so be prepared to jostle with the crowds for a photograph.

Built by King Anourat (r. 1791-1817), it was restored in 1914. From here a procession starts at Lao New Year. Various legends are attached to the mount, including one of hidden treasure. A monk was said to have found the treasure in a deep pit but it was seized by villagers and the monk buried alive in the pit. However, magical charms enabled the monk to extricate himself. When the king heard of the treachery, he punished the villagers by ordering them to beat drums, gongs and cymbals every three hours to prevent mythical dragons from disturbing mankind.

An old photo showing That Chomsi on Mount Phousi at the very top of the picture

That Chomsi remains one of the prominent landmarks of Luang Prabang.

Wat Mai Suwannaphumaham

Location: Sisavangvong Road (Photthisarat Road according to some maps).
Date: 1788
Restored 1943 and 1963.
Style: Luang Prabang Style I

*** Highlight**
Verandah with golden bas-relief

This is one of the grandest and most impressive temples in Luang Prabang. It has a dramatic five-tiered red roof with a verandah at either end, projecting with its own pitched roof at right angles to the main roof. The eastern, main verandah has a lavishly decorated doorway, ceiling and supporting pillars, covered with gilded and stencilled columns and golden painted stucco bas-reliefs. The main roof is topped with a small *dok so faa* of three golden parasols.

The temple, close to the Royal Palace, was inaugurated in 1788 (although some historians say it was 1794) having taken 70 years to complete, and housed the golden Pra Bang Buddha, palladium of Luang Prabang, between 1894 and 1947. Wat Mai means 'New Monastery' and it was here that the Pra Sangkharat, the highest Buddhist dignitary in Laos, resided from 1894. There are old photographs of him on the altar with flowers and candles, showing how much he is still revered. Restoration took place in 1821 during the reign of King Manthatourat (1817-36). During the reign of King Oun Kham (1872-87), his son Sakkarine ordered the construction of the east and west verandahs. The golden stucco work was done in 1968.

Wat Mai viewed from the side. Note the unusual five-tiered roof.

The front verandah.

An early woodblock print by Louis Delaporte, shows Wat Mai surrounded by lush trees and vegetation on an unpaved road with local people strolling alongside a water buffalo with two children riding on it, and lots of chickens.

During new year celebrations, the golden Pra Bang Buddha is brought from the Royal Palace to Wat Mai for its annual three day ritual ablutions.

The star attraction of Wat Mai is its verandah. It has a carmine painted ceiling decorated with vivid gold *dharma* wheels and floral motifs. There are beams and cross-beams in gilded stucco with carved scenes from the *Phra Lak Phra Lam,* as well as many highly detailed images of gods and animals from the signs of the zodiac. The demon king is shown as a giant crab, waving its claws to attack the monkey general Hanuman. This structure is supported by 12 jet black Corinthian-style wood columns covered with gold stencils of delicate abstract designs, crowned with capitals of gilded lotus petals. The eave brackets are carved in the shape of gold *nagas.*

Aerial photo of Wat Mai Suwannaphumaham.

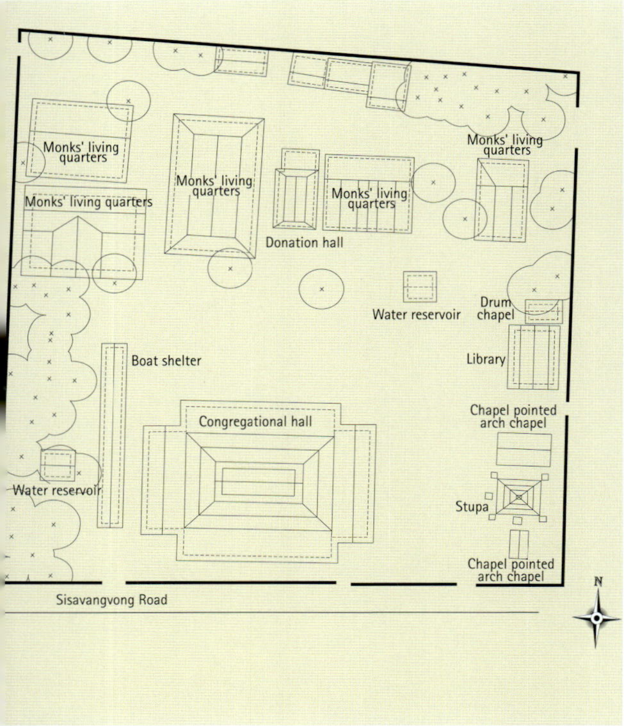

Top: *A print of Wat Mai Suwannaphumaham by Louis Delaporte.*

Wat Mai in the past. This is one of the rare cases where the temple remains almost unchanged in both the construction and decoration.
(Courtesy University of Illinois)

The superb golden bas-reliefs around the main entrance, executed in the 1960s, are also filled with extraordinary detail, including the *Vessantara Jataka,* the story of the last reincarnation of the historic Buddha. Sacred images of the Buddha in a heavenly palace and in a holy chariot are shown above. The physical appearance of the deities enhance the most attractive aspects of the human body, with the Buddha dressed like a king, *bodhisattvas* resembling princes, and goddesses like bejewelled royal consorts. These are interspersed with lively vignettes of daily life below, showing simple wooden houses on stilts, their occupants sitting outside. Village women are depicted wearing their *phaa sin,* a hip wrapper, naked above the waist, going about their work, carrying baskets and water pots from the river. At the base of the bas-relief are images of farm animals such as water buffalo and pigs, as well as elephants, tigers and a bear. The people and animals are shown in an idyllic golden landscape of mango trees and swaying palms. Heaven and earth appear juxtaposed, as the heavenly realm resembles the perfect human world, filled with happiness and devoid of suffering, while the earthly realm is like paradise, so the sacred becomes mundane and the mundane sacred.

The interior of the *sim* has a huge Buddha statue and is an amalgam of gold and crimson.

In the compound is a covered structure housing two longboats used for the religious boat races in Lao New Year.

Following pages: *The verandah with its wealth of gold stucco decoration.* (PP)

Opposite: *Door of the* sim. (PP)

Below: *Detail of the* sim *façade. This is the work of Pae Ton, who has been honoured as a national artist.* (PP)

The principal Buddha image of Wat Mai. Near the altar there is a sculpture of Phra Sangkharat. (OC)

Opposite: *Scenes from* Phra Lak Phra Lam. *The monkey army* (top left). *Hanuman fighting with Totsakan as a giant crab* (top right).

Location: Photthisarat Road
Date: 1705
Style: Luang Prabang Style I

*** Highlight**
Silver nagas

Wat Ho Xieng

The so-called Lottery Pavilion was named after a ceremony with King Setthathirat (r. 1548-71) in 1548. It was founded in 1705 by Sene Mu Xa, and destroyed in 1900 during a storm. It was rebuilt in 1973.

Now newly renovated, the *sim* has a three-tiered roof with gilded *cho faa* rearing upwards at the end of each tier. Four octagonal gilded and red columns with lotus petal capitals support the roof, while the outer periphery has low rectangular columns with eave brackets in the form of golden *nagas.* The tympanum of the gable has mosaics and an unusual image of Rama, bedecked in gold and wearing a pointed crown, standing in the centre. The image is set against an abstract patterned background. There is a gilded wood Buddha image holding a bowl at his chest, also unusual in Lao iconography. The single portico has two panels featuring an image of Rama standing in balletic pose on a mythical animal. The central stairway has flamboyant three headed silver *nagas.*

Naga *as eave brackets along the side of the* sim. (OC)

The sim *of Wat Ho Xieng.*

Wat Phra Mahathat (Wat That)

Location: Photthisarat Road adjacent to Wat Ho Xieng.
Date: Built in 1548 but restored at the start of 20th century and then renovated in 1991.
Style: Luang Prabang Style I

Built during reign of King Setthathirat (1548-71) it collapsed during a storm in 1900 and was rebuilt between 1907-1910, under *Oupahat* Boun Khong. It was then restored in 1963 and 1991.

This temple is of great importance during New Year. On the third day, when the tutelary deity of the year arrives, the monks of Wat Xieng Thong, Wat Mai, Wat Aham and Wat Visoun are brought by ceremonial palanquins in a procession to attend the sacred dance of Pu No and Na No, the guardian spirits of Luang Prabang.

This is an extravagant temple with many shrines and stupas. The *sim* has a peripheral verandah and ornate doors and windows with golden figures from the *Ramayana.* On the verandah six black and gold columns, four tall and two short, support a sweeping, heavy looking two-tiered tiled roof. Five small staircases leading up into the *wat,* two on each side and a main staircase at the eastern principal portico, they are all decorated with dramatic five-headed silver *nagas.* Seven eave brackets are in the form of golden *nagas,* their single heads rearing up. At the top of the ornately gilded gable is a *dharma* wheel. The multiple parasols of the *dok so faa* show that this was built for a king. The large three-tiered black stupa dates from the 16th century.

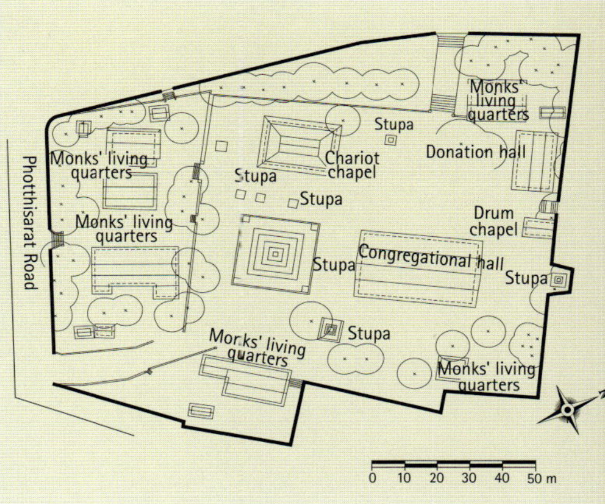

The temple in the past.
(Courtesy the University of Illinois)

The sim *with the black stupa behind.*

Opposite: *The entrance of the* sim *has a pediment with a* dharma *wheel surmounted by a seven-tiered parasol. Note the mural painted on the wall of the verandah.*

Gold nagas on the eave brackets of the sim *similar to Wat Ho Xieng.* (OC)

The ornate doors and windows are carved with golden figures from the Phra Lak Phra Lam. *The main door panels depict Rama, on the right, with a face of great refinement, holding his bow and arrows in his right hand while his left hand touches his heart. Beside him is the golden deer, Marica, which his beloved Sita has begged him to bring her. On the left panel Sita kneels as wicked Ravana approaches her in the guise of a holy ascetic. The composition of these door panels is exceptionally fine. Facing east, and often in shadow, they are best seen in the early morning when the sun picks out the gold.*

Location: Souvannabanlang Road
Date: 1791
Style: Luang Prabang Style III

Wat Phone Say (Phonexay)

This temple was built in 1791 by King Anourat (r. 1791-1817) and named after the Buddha sculpture it once housed. Kings would pray here before departing for war.

It was rebuilt to a simple plan in reinforced concrete in 1970. The sim has a front and two lateral verandahs. Now recently restored once more, it has a garish red and gold gable whose upper part depicts a seated Buddha image surrounded by foliage. Below are two further Buddha images with kneeling disciples. Perhaps because of its rebuilding Wat Phone Say lacks the subtle artistry found elsewhere in Luang Prabang. Lurid murals in primary colours are painted in a rustic style and depict the life of the Buddha. Still more dramatic are the rather unsophisticated but startling murals showing the horrors of hell – people are sawn in half, chopped up, strangled, hanged and beheaded. However, what they achieve in didactic terms perhaps compensates for what they lack artistically. To complete the ensemble, two monstrous lions guard the main entrance.

The front of the sim.

Mural paintings on the front facade showing pictures of hell.

An old photo of the front facade.(Courtesy University of Illinois)

Location: Photthisarat Road
Date: 17th century
Style: Luang Prabang Style

*** Highlight**
Buddha footprint
Sunset views

WAT PHRA BAT TAI (WAT PHABATHAY)

This was originally a wood temple which dated back to the 17th century, known as Wat Keo. Colloquially, the word *Keo* designates Vietnamese people. Wat Phra Bat Tai is honoured by the small Vietnamese community of Luang Prabang as their temple, and services are in Vietnamese and Lao.

This site is older and dates to the period when Fa Ngum (1353-73) was enthroned and Khmer Buddhist monks came to Luang Prabang from Angkor, bearing, according to some accounts, the Pra Bang Buddha statue. The monks asked to build a monastery near the confluence of the rivers Mekong and Nam Khan on a rock where one of the city's 15 *naga* protectors was said to have resided. The arrival of these Khmer monks marks the official introduction of Buddhism to Lane Xang.

The *sim* was burnt down in 1833. Most of the present structure was rebuilt in the 19th century by the local Vietnamese and Chinese communities. The Vietnamese name of the temple is Chua Phat Tich. It is more Vietnamese in style and the aesthetics differs from the more restrained Lao taste. Brightly painted in primary blue and sunburst yellow, with numerous hanging lights, it looks almost carnivalesque, and, in keeping with such a theme there is fortune telling at the entrance. Fortune tellers have always been consulted in Lao society and a reading is normally based on the birthday of the supplicant. However this particular method does not require a fortune teller. Instead the person seeking an answer kneels down and shakes a bamboo tube containing bamboo sticks in both hands until one of the sticks falls out. The number on the stick relates to the prediction printed on a piece of paper.

There is a huge Buddha footprint, an important object of veneration, in the grounds, and at the far western end of the *wat* there are steps leading to the Mekong. This is an ideal spot to watch the sunset.

Opposite below: *The gate to Wat Phra Bat Tai makes clear that the style of this temple is unlike any others in Luang Prabang.*

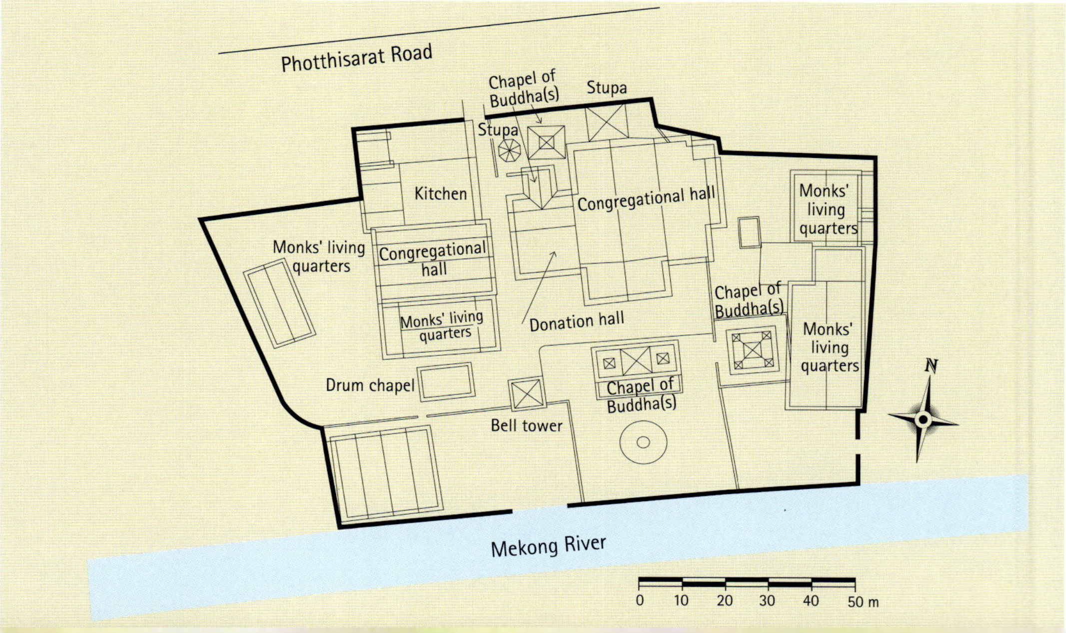

Buddha footprint in a small chapel at the back of the temple by the river.

Paper predictions and bamboo tube with sticks for fortune telling.

Location: Close to Wat Phra Mahathat, in an adjacent compound.
Date: 1818
Style: Luang Prabang Style III

*** Highlight**
Window shutters depicting gold and silver divinities

Opposite above: *Lotus capitals and decoration on the gable of the* sim. (OC)

Opposite below: *Door panels showing a scene from* Phra Lak Phra Lam (left) *and window panels showing deities in the* lalitasana *pose* (right).

Wat That Luang

Built on a low hill by King Manthatourat (r. 1817-36), the temple has a *sim* and two large stupas. The *sim* is purported to have been built from a banyan tree which once grew close to Wat Keo. This is the Monastery of the Royal Stupa, located in the southern part of the town close to the older monasteries. Before 1975, it was the place of cremation for the members of the royal family.

Wat That Luang was located in a large open stretch of land where these royal cremations were held, as well as annual ceremonies. Regrettably a petrol station now stands on one corner.

This whitewashed temple has a two-tiered roof. Its silhouette is unusual as the higher roof, with its *dok so faa* of 15 parasols, denoting royal status, posed on a gold and red base, has a decorated tympanum above the lower roof, which then sweeps down and is supported by slender eave brackets. There are three doors at either end and two doors and four windows on each side. Although the simple white staircases have little decoration, except for low newel posts in the form of lotus buds, the windows and doors are especially noteworthy.

Wat That Luang, the site where the royal family gathers annually on 29 October to commemorate King Sisavangvong.

The doors are painted with silver mythological figures on a black background, and the deeply recessed window shutters with figures in gold on black. Some show Rama in combat with the demon Ravana, a scene from the *Phra Lak Phra Lam.* On another panel, the upper figure holds an uprooted tree, its roots hanging down. One fine window panel depicts two balletic looking bejewelled female divinities, with bracelets, necklaces and anklets, sitting in the *lalitasana* position, crosslegged with one leg hanging down, on lotus thrones. It is unusual to find the *lalitasana* pose in Lao art. Each has two sets of arms and wears a pointed crown framed by a similarly shaped radiance or halo, and is surrounded by a design of swirling golden motifs. The upper hands hold a *dharma* wheel and a conch shell, an auspicious symbol of prosperity, the lower hands a flaming torch and a three pointed trident, emblems of destruction. Such Hindu imagery is associated with Vishnu, suggesting that the goddess, possibly Durga, is the female energy of Vishnu, protecting the temple. Below each of them are single *nagas,* curled into figure eights.

The next window shows a slender and elegant female divinity wrapped in a *phaa sin,* a sarong, on a lotus stand, with an elephant below. The adjoining panel depicts a deity holding a staff and balancing on a mythical lion.

The stupas here include a gold stupa on the eastern side of the *sim* that holds the ashes of King Sisavangvong (r. 1904-59), whose funeral hearse is in Wat Xieng Thong. It was renovated in the 1960s.

A large dark grey, almost black, stupa has an elegant curved shape on a stepped square base, finished with a single spiral parasol. In Buddhist cosmology the pillar is the *axis mundi,* the world mountain, pivot of the universe, and the umbrella an honorific and auspicious emblem. The monument would contain sacred relics and, for protection, geometric and magical designs would be placed around it. There are square blue tiles on the lower base, some bearing the swastika symbol. These point alternately clockwise and anticlockwise. The swastika, from the Sanskri *svasti,* represents the sun and its energy. The arms of the swastika point in the cardinal directions. When the sign appears to rotate clockwise, it symbolises the positive and creative energy of the sun. The anti-clockwise swastika refers to autumn and the winter sun and is considered unlucky. Similar motifs appear in Wat Pa Khe.

Left: *Two old photos showing the stupa before* (top) *and after restoration. Artefacts found therein are now kept in the museum.* (Courtesy University of Illinois)

Opposite: *Window panels depict a female divinity wearing a* phaa sin *and a male heavenly figure holding an arrow.*

Location: Photthisarat Road
Date: The site is thought to be the oldest in the city, dating from 14th century. The temple was reconstructed in 1818, burned down in 1887 and rebuilt in 1972.
Style: Luang Prabang Style III

Wat Monorom (Wat Manorom)

This extensive temple complex was built by the nobles of Luang Prabang. It was intended for the ashes of King Sam Saentai (r. 1373-1416), son of King Fa Ngum (r. 1353-73). It contained a celebrated bronze Buddha in the Siamese Sukhothai style, cast in the 1370s during King Sam Saentai's reign, six metres high and said to have weighed 12 tons, but it was destroyed in 1887 when the town was plundered. Although armless, it was restored and raised again in 1919. In 1971 it was repaired with cement and lacquered and painted with gold leaf. According to Henri Parmentier, this particular bronze sculpture was a seminal influence on Lao artists.

It contains a large square gold stupa, almost a reproduction of the That Luang in Vientiane and hosts many different festivals. It is currently being renovated.

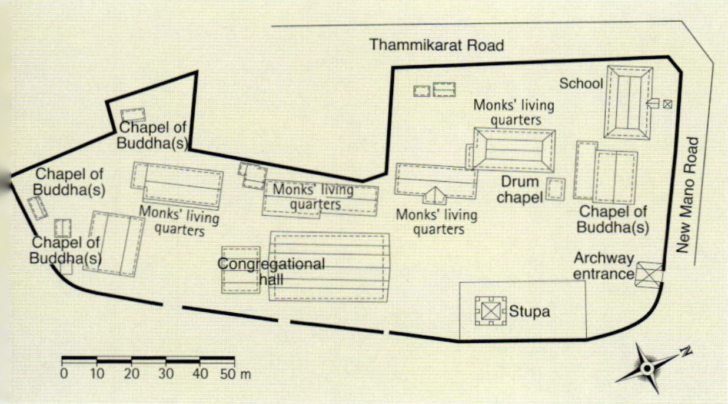

Gold stupa, whose shape is similar to Phra That Luang in Vientiane and is unique to Laos.

The remains of the colossal bronze Buddha that was burned down in 1887.
(Courtesy University of Illinois)

The 1972 rebuilt sim *constructed from donations.* (OC)

The Buddha statue cast from the old one on the previous page.

Lions guarding the side entrance of the sim.

Detail of the mural on the front façade of the sim. (OC)

The impressively large main *sim* has a three tiered roof with finials, six octagonal red and gold columns at the verandah, in descending size, with gold lotus petal capitals, while each side has ten more columns. On the central part of the gable is a seated Buddha with foliated scrolls spreading out below and around him. There are brightly painted contemporary murals illustrating the lives of the Buddha, covering the main façade. The building has finely carved doors with projecting lintels and a painted ceiling. On the northern side the entrance is guarded by two rather flamboyant mythical gold lions, their mouths wide open and their tails curling over their backs, their bodies decorated with designs of swirling gold.

Memorial plaques to the dead installed by their relatives and carved with their names and dates.

Wat Visounnarat (Wat Vixoun, Wat Visoun)

Location: Visounnarat Road
Date: Orginally 1503, according to Parmentier, rebuilt 1898.
Style: Luang Prabang Style I

Founded in 1512, during the reign of King Visounnarat (1501-1520), although some historians say it was built during the reign of King Photthisarat (1520-48), this temple was a symbol of the kingdom's unity. An early woodblock print by Louis Delaporte shows a much more ornate temple with sloping walls, built between 1512-1515.

It was constructed with timber from northern Laos. Some 4,000 trees were used, according to legend, with the main roof being supported by 12 pillars, 30 metres high, each said to be a tree from a different forest. The *wat* is said to be close to the rice fields of the *devata luang,* the tutelary spirits, Pu No and Na No. It was destroyed by fire in 1887 following attacks by Chinese marauders. In 1898, during the reign of King Sakkarine Khamsouk (1894-1904), it was rebuilt. It was here that the revered gold Pra Bang Buddha was kept between 1513 and 1707, after which it was kept in Vientiane. It was brought back here between 1867 and 1887, but the *wat* was then burned down in an attack. It was rebuilt in 1898.

A print by Delaporte of Wat Visoun before it was destroyed by fire. (Courtesy White Lotus)

The temple at present has a much plainer sim.

Wooden gilded door panel depicting Shiva on the bull Nandi. Vishnu, Bhrama and Indra can be seen on other door panels.

The simple whitewashed exterior of the rebuilt *sim* belies the importance of this temple which today is a veritable museum of religious art, housing one of the most important collection of Buddha images. Several ancient Khmer pieces have been removed to the National Museum (the former Royal Palace).

The temple with its rectangular two tiered roof is a replica of the original wooden building constructed in 1512 by King Visounnarat. The windows were recreated like the originals, with carved rounded balusters of Khmer style, resembling those in stone at Angkor, and the doors are finely carved with images of Shiva and Vishnu. When the temple burned down the door panels depicting Vishnu and Shiva, Brahma and Indra, were saved and reinstated here. The *sim* has a high ceiling. Look up in the interior to see the intricate construction of the wat and the superbly carved beams, some decorated with gold stencils.

There is an enormous Buddha statue in the centre, the largest in the city, with stylised tightly curled hair and long ears, together with old stelae that are engraved with *hiu chaluk*, Pali scriptures. Behind the altar, arranged on shelves, is a fine collection of Buddha statues accumulated by Prince Phetsarath (1890-1959, *see Xiengkeo Mansion*) who chose this as a repository. The statues, some of which are 400 years old, are dusty and stacked up rather haphazardly at the far southern end of the *wat*. They include kneeling and standing buddhas, many in the *mudra* of calling for rain, but also in the *abayamudra*, dispelling fear or giving protection and the *dhyanamudra,* meditation position. Many of these have, sadly, disappeared over the last few years.

Look at the carved *Ramayana* screen, early 20th century, with coloured with coloured glass inlay. It shows the battle of the white monkey Hanuman with the black monkey Nilaphar during the building of the stone bridge to Lanka. At the top is Sugriva, trying to intervene amid the melee of fighting monkeys.

This shows the monkey army with Hanuman the White Monkey fighting with Nilaphar, the Black Monkey, with Sugriva, their king, at the top. He is angry at their quarrel and trying to separate them during the construction of the dyke across the water that would permit Rama's army to invade the island of Lanka. The scene reveals the frenzied melèe of monkeys while, below, several of them attack the raksasas *who were guarding Lanka.* (PP)

Gilded wooden Buddha statues line the corridor in the sim.

Buddha images crowd the main altar in the sim*,*
as in other temples in the town.

Location: Phommathat Road, adjacent to Wat Visoun, through the archway.
Date: 1503-4, rebuilt 1898
Style: Stupa with hemispherical dome.

Opposite: *The Watermelon stupa. During the restoration of 1932, one of the artefacts found was a miniature golden stupa which is now housed in the Royal Palace Museum.*

In the foreground is the archway connecting Wat Aham and Wat Visoun. It is the oldest of its kind in Luang Prabang.
(Courtesy University of Illinois)

Wat Thakmo (That Pathum)

This 35 metre high grey Lotus Stupa built of masonry is known as the Watermelon Stupa because of its stylised hemispherical dome, *anda.* Set in a picturesque setting of tall palm trees, it is built on a stepped square base with small stupas at each of the cardinal points to symbolise the four elements.

Displaying Sinhalese (Sri Lanka) influence, it was built by Queen Visounnarat (whose husband King Visounnarat reigned 1501-1520) in 1504, although the École Française d'Éxtrême-Orient claims it was 1514. It was filled with Buddha images which were stolen by Chinese raiders in 1887 when Wat Visoun was destroyed. It was rebuilt in 1898, and collapsed in 1914, apparently having been struck by lightning. The damage revealed 179 pieces of treasure within, including 15th and 16th century gold, bronze and crystal Buddhas images, which were removed to the National Museum for safekeeping. Restoration work was carried out in 1932.

Detail of the sim *verandah at Wat Aham with its typical Luang Prabang decorative motifs.*

The front of the sim *at Wat Aham is guarded by two lions and Hanuman and Ravana from* Phra Lak Phra Lam. (OC)

Wat Aphay

Location: Phommathat Road, opposite Wat Aham.
Date: 1527
Style: Luang Prabang Style III

Children play in the dusty compound here where the *wat* is under renovation. It was built in the reign of King Photthisarat (1520-1548) by a merchant of pickled fish, *pla-dak*. Originally it was called Wat Hai Pai Pla Dak. In 1923, during restoration, the name was changed to Wat Aphay. The tympanum of the western gable of the two-tiered *sim* has an image of the three-headed elephant, Indra's mount Erawan, and symbol of the former kingdom of Lane Xang, Land of a Million Elephants.

A distinctive feature of the *sim* is the cloister with murals depicting stories of the Buddha Maitreya. The gilded stupa, a future Buddha, a *bodhisattva* who will appear on earth. in Lan Na style, is topped with a parasol.

A Buddha statue in bhumisparsamudra. *Note the small figure in front. This is the Earth Goddess, Nang Thorani (from Sanskrit* dharani, *the earth), she wrings water from her hair to vanquish the demon Mara's army which attempted to stop the Buddha from meditating.*

Back view of the sim.

Location Chao Xomphou Road
Date: 1533
Style: Luang Prabang Style III

*** Highlight**
Ornate lintel

WAT MEUNNA (MEUN NA)

Built under King Photthisarat (r. 1520-48) in 1533, it was named Monastery of Ten Thousand Rice Fields. A *meun* is a unit of weight, about 12 kilos, given by each villager when the temple was built.

The white washed *sim* has a three-tiered roof, with a *dok so faa* of nine parasols. There are five white rectangular columns on either side. The eastern main entrance has four renovated hexagonal gold and red decorated columns. The elaborately gilded doorway has an ornate lintel with consecutive rising carvings. The walls, both inside and outside the verandah are covered with rather rustic, 'primitive' style contemporary murals in primary colours of blue, red and yellow showing the lives of the Buddha and a deity in prayer on a three-headed elephant. These realistic representations make up in devotional inspiration what they lack in artistic merit. It was restored in 1920 and two lateral galleries were added to the *sim.*

Side view of the temple showing the sweeping roof and the typical form of Luang Prabang's cho faa.

Above left and right: *Brightly painted murals on the front facade of the* sim *illustrate the life of the Buddha.*

Below left and right: *The side chapel is used as a place to store old Buddha images.* (Old photo courtesy University of Illinois)

Location: On road to airport.
Date: Completed 1988.
Style: Modelled on the Shwedagon Pagoda in Rangoon.

Wat Phra Phome Phao Santi Chedi

The bell-shaped stupa atop an octagonal structure with verandahs can be seen gleaming in the sunshine across the Nam Khan river, three kilometres east of Luang Prabang. This simple forest style *wat* is plain and unadorned, but looks evocative from a distance as its thin golden spire and hexagonal roof rise amid the misty forest around it. The interior walls are covered with brightly painted frescoes of the Buddhist heavens and hells, especially lurid in their depictions of the brutalities of the latter.

The *wat* was built with donations from Lao people living abroad, and started in 1959 although not finished until 1988. On the pillars inside are inscribed the names of the donors.

The shape of the Phome Phao Santi Chedi is unusual.

The temple is located on a bend of the Nam Khan river.

Wat Sankhalok

Location: 6 kilometres south of Luang Prabang
Date: Rebuilt 1905
Style: Luang Prabang Style II

An important centre for the New Year festivities and the Pu No and Na No ceremonial dances.

According to historians, this temple, built on marshes where a legendary dragon lived, is said to occupy the earliest Buddhist site in Luang Prabang occupied by the Khmers during the period of the Khmer empire. Five stone Buddha statues were discovered near the *wat* dating to two centuries before Fa Ngum. These images reflect the Mahayana branch of Buddhism that prevailed at Angkor at various periods during the 11th and 12th centuries. It was originally built in 1527 by King Photthisarat, and restored in 1909. It has a verandah and three naves.

Below: *The* sim *with three-headed elephant, symbol of Luang Prabang, and* nagas. (OC)

Below left: *Stupa at the back of the* sim. (OC)

The sim and *stupa in the past.* (Courtesy University of Illinois)

Location: Far side of the river
Date: 19th century
Style: Luang Prabang Style II

*** Highlight**
Elaborate gilded doorway

Wat Xiang Men

The name of the temple means Heavenly City (of Muang Men). According to the inscription found under the main altar in the *sim,* the temple was built during the reign of King Setthathirat (1548-71) and was later under the royal patronage of Setthathirat's son, Woraratthamprachod.

The *sim* has a three-tiered roof supported by six red and gold octagonal columns. Its small size indicates that it is Luang Prabang II style. The stucco entrance of the *sim* is embellished with a gilded *naga* and a *hamsa* and is the most decorative part of the temple. Inside the *sim,* the round columns are covered with gold stencils and the wall behind the main altar is painted gold.

To reach the temple, the visitor takes a boat from the main pier. The trip lasts about 15 minutes and is followed by a pleasant walk through the village to the temple.

Opposite top: *The Buddha statue in the* sim. (OC)

Below: *The sim with the sweeping roof line, typical of Luang Prabang.* (OC)

Opposite below right: *An embroidered cloth depicting the Buddha is said by the monks to be 300 years old.* (OC)

Opposite below left: *Ornate decoration demarcates the entrance to the* sim. (OC)

Location: On a hilltop on the other side of the river. Reached by 100 steep steps.
Date: Possibly 18th century
Style: Luang Prabang Style II

*** Highlight**
Ceiling stencils

Wat Chom Phet

This delightful and contemplative *wat*, with its two-tiered roof, recently restored, is worth the climb for its outstanding crimson painted ceiling, both above the verandah and within the *sim.* The ceiling is decorated with enchanting gold stencilled images of scampering mice, butterflies, lovebirds, bees, peacocks, mythical animals and delicate floral and feather patterns. There are four white undecorated cylindrical columns with just one red portico on the cracked eastern façade.

The door is surmounted by a gilded stucco pediment on which two tiny Buddha amulets and two miniscule human figures are almost buried within the flowers and foliage. It has a triangular shaped gilded stucco carving over it, with tightly packed leaves and flowers, mostly lotus blossoms, with two tiny Buddha amulets and two miniscule human figures almost buried within the flower images, and a lotus at the top.

The temple has been restored and the beautiful stencils on the ceiling make the trip across the Mekong worthwhile.

Delightful animals and birds are stencilled in gold on the red ceiling.

Wat Long Khoun

Location: A journey by ferry to the west bank of the Mekong.
Date: 18th century. Restored by the École Française d'Extrême-Orient in 1994.
Style: Luang Prabang Style III

*** Highlight**
Painted guardian figures in Chinese style

A former centre for royal retreats, the temple is reached by ferry to the west bank of the Mekong. After disembarking, steps lead up to the temple, the finest of a group of three on this side of the river. Meditation buildings in the compound were intended for use by the kings and monks on special occasions.

The compound measures 1.5 hectares. The *sim* has a simple roof with a lower one over the porch supported by eight black and gold hexagonal columns. Restored under the aegis of Lao architect Madame Sounantha Kattiyasack, it has especially noteworthy murals on the exterior. The front porch was added in 1937.

On either side of the sculpted entrance to the *sim* are painted two Chinese gentlemen of great stylistic interest with beards, elaborate costumes and hats. In colours of pale washed-out aquamarine and terracotta, their figures are rather portly but stand erect and commanding. Their faces are strong and dignified, with slanting eyes and eyebrows, bushy beards painted almost whisker by whisker, and ornate small hats. Each carries on his back what appears to be a sword, with just the hilt visible above the shoulder. Their hands are elegantly tapered, suggesting gentlemen of leisure,

Wat Long Khoun. In the past kings would spend three days here before attending the coronation ceremony at Wat Xieng Thong.

The side view of the sim *with the front porch which was added in 1937.*

Detail of mural below.

Two bearded Chinese gentlemen of great stylistic interest, with elaborate costumes and hats not dissimilar to crowns worn by Chinese and Vietnamese emperors.

Murals inside the sim *illustrate* jataka *tales.*

and each holds a handkerchief, with supple folds suggestive of silk. The costumes appear to be those of a warrior, or perhaps even a wealthy merchant, with bows at the neck, two-tone sleeves with a flounce at the elbow, trousers that could be armour, and low slung belts tied at the side.

Above these two impressive figures is a red painted wooden ceiling covered with gold stencilled *dharma* wheels, mythical animals, monkeys, butterflies and peacocks. It is supported by eight hexagonal black and gold columns with gold lotus petal capitals columns. The murals inside the sim are more traditionally Lao in style, depicting *jataka* tales.

Stencils on the ceiling are similar to Wat Chom Phet.

Wat Tham

Location: This is upstream about 100 metres from Wat Long Khoun.
Date: Ancient
Style: Cave Monastery

Caves have long been revered as sacred places and consequently have often been transformed into depositories for Buddha images. Local children can obtain a key and torch and will guide visitors inside. The tenebrous, dark limestone cave has a stupa and many old Buddha images, some quite decayed, which would benefit from restoration and safekeeping.

Above: *The key to the cave is kept by local children.*
Above right: *Stupa inside the temple.*
Right: *Abandoned Buddha images inside the temple.*

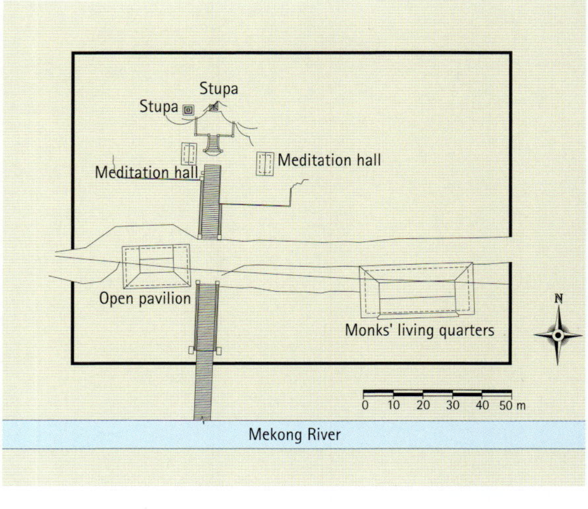

Location: 25 kilometres upriver from Luang Prabang are the sacred caves of Pak Ou, in the limestone cliffs.
Date: 16th century
Style: Cave monastery

Pak Ou Caves

Located in limestone cliffs 25 kilometres upriver from Luang Prabang, the caves are said to have been discovered by King Setthathirat (r. 1520-48) in the 16th century, after the construction of Wat Pak Ou, on the other bank of the river at Ban Pak Ou, but they were possibly centres of spirit worship prior to this time. The king visited every New Year, and would have stayed on the other bank of the Mekong, at Ban Pak Ou. Francis Garnier, the French explorer, visited the caves on his travels when he charted the Mekong river in the 1860s.

Both the upper and lower limestone cliffs have caves, connected by steep steps, and filled with Buddhas statues. This is a place of pilgrimage, a numinous journey, and pilgrims have come here for centuries. They believe that *phi,* the spirits of the rivers and cave, dwell here.

The caves are set high in a cliff that rises vertically from the Mekong river, and they are reached by a series of steep steps. There are two levels, and the caves are called, respectively, Tham Thing and the upper ones Tham Phum. The higher ones are some 60 metres above the river. The lower cave is the focal point for

An old photo of the cave during an annual festival.

Swathes of limestone hang down at the entrance to the Pak Ou caves.

most visitors. Offerings of flowers and incense are made here, and local villagers sell these on the steps going up. Images of lions guard the entrance to the caves.

At New Year crowds of people flock to the caves by boat from Luang Prabang. Inside there are thousands of historic Buddha statues, brought by pilgrims over the centuries. Most date from the 18th and 19th centuries. The older ones, covered with dust, are of wood, predominantly in the style of the Buddha Calling for Rain, but also a variety of other poses, including Calling the Earth to Witness and Meditation *mudras.* Some are tiny, a few centimetres high, while others are much taller. Lacquered and gilded, many are dilapidated, but their dust-covered appearance, all crammed together in the caves, makes for a haunting atmosphere that lingers in the memory. Official figures placed the number of images in the region of 4,000, and they used to fill every shelf and crevice of the caves. Unfortunately many have been stolen and are increasingly being replaced by modern plaster ones.

A woman at Pak Ou caves selling flowers, joss sticks and candles as offerings to the Buddha images.

Buddha statues have been deposited in the caves over many years by lay people.

Above: *Lions guarding Pak Ou caves.*
Above left: *Buddha sculptures in Pak Ou caves.*

Getting There:

Leaving Luang Prabang by local boat, you take a picturesque two hour boat ride on the wide river, past sheer limestone cliffs and banks of graceful bamboo and palm trees, that brings you to Pak Ou on the western bank of the river. Look out for the different colours in the swirling waters as the Nam Khan tributary reaches the Mekong river. The waters of the Mekong are a beige, toffee colour, and the Nam Khan is darker.

Long-tail boats to Pak Ou caves.

Khouang Sy Waterfalls

Khouang Sy Waterfall is 32 km south-west of Luang Prabang are the delightful Khouang Sy waterfalls, surrounded by lush tropical vegetation. These are not dramatic falls, although heavier cascades of water occur after the rainy season, but they are picturesque. The water tumbles over limestone formations and collects in aquamarine pools. These can be reached via winding paths to the left, culminating in higher pools above the principal falls. The natural beauty of the setting offers a refreshing and bucolic outing after temple visiting.

Khouang Sy Waterfalls.

The Living Land

Just beyond the Khouang Sy Waterfalls is a community project, a living rice farm called The Living Land. Visitors can spend a half day in idyllic countryside, surrounded by mountains, in the middle of ancient rice terraces. Supporting the local community and helping to educate children from disadvantaged farming families, The Living Land is a community enterprise, growing organic vegetables and rice. Every conceivable vegetable, salad and herb grows abundantly in row after row of variegated greens. Visitors can participate in demonstrations of every stage of rice growing, harvesting and winnowing, assisting buffaloes using ploughs and pressing sugar cane juice. For the more sedate, it can all be viewed from the balcony of a traditional Lao rice house.

Visits can be booked at The Living Rice Farm, telephone 020 551 99208. Website: www.livinglandlao.com

HENRI MOUHOT'S TOMB

Above: *Plaque donated by the town of Montbéliard, France (birthplace of Mouhot) at his tomb in Luang Prabang.* (RB)

Below: *The tomb of Henri Mouhot outside Luang Prabang.*

The tomb of Henri Mouhot (1826-1861) is on a steep, verdant bank of the Nam Khan, outside Luang Prabang. His expedition of 1860 continued after his discovery of Angkor and he travelled up the Mekong and rode by elephant deep into the jungles of Laos. He died of malaria the following year, on November 10 1861, aged only 35.

His isolated tomb was forgotten and overgrown, until it was rediscovered in 1990 by a French writer and Lao guide *(see Brief History).* It is 15 kilometres from Luang Prabang, close to the village of Ban Panom.

Ock Pop Tok Weaving Centre.

Ock Pop Tok The Living Craft Centre

Another enterprising project to enable visitors to learn about Lao textiles and handicrafts and to promote creative artisans. Ock Pop Tok, (meaning East meets West) is set in a tropical Mekong riverside garden where silk weavers and craft artisans demonstrate their skills in a Living Craft Centre.

The company was started in 2000 by a local weaver and an English photographer, Joanne Smith. Their philosophy was to empower women through their traditional skills and to advance the artistic, cultural and social development of Lao artisans, as well as promoting Laotian textiles around the world.

Guided tours of looms, dyeing with vegetable dyes, basket and bamboo weaving, batik drawing and other crafts as well as witnessing living silkworms and viewing changing exhibitions in their gallery space can all be arranged, culminating in a delicious Lao meal in their river view Silk Road café. They also have two fair-trade shops in Luang Prabang.

Two kilometres south-west of Luang Prabang, in Ban Saylom, on the road to Khouang Sy waterfalls.

Tel: (856) 071-212597 Email: lcc@ockpoptok.com

Web Site :www.ockpoptok.com

THE ROYAL PALACE (THE NATIONAL MUSEUM)

The Royal Palace

"The princes … displayed for my benefit all they could devise of pomp and splendour."
Henri Mouhot

The gable of the Royal Palace with a symbol of the Lane Xang kingdom. (PP)

Opposite: *Palm trees line the path to the palace.*

Overleaf: *New shrine for Pra Bang Buddha at The Royal Palace.*

The Royal Palace, was known as the *Ho Kham,* Golden Palace, and is now the National Museum. It was built between 1904-1909, replacing a wooden palace which was demolished. The palace, commissioned and designed by the French colonial administration, symbolised the liaison between France and Laos. It is a blend of the French *beaux arts* style and Lao vernacular architecture.

The former palace faced the river, but the new construction faced the sacred Mount Phousi, opening out on to the main street, Photthisarat Road, via an avenue of majestic palm trees. Viewed from the top of nearby Mount Phousi, the grandeur of the palace can be better appreciated. It is set among verdant gardens close to the Mekong river from where royal guests arrived by barge at a disembarkation point and ascended a stairway leading to the palace grounds.

An old banyan tree stands in the palace compound.

Top: *The back of the Royal Palace shows the fusion between eastern and western styles.*

There is a large pond in the grounds.

Alix de Fautereau

The walls in The King's Reception Room, or Audience Room, are covered with large paintings dating from 1930 by French painter Alix de Fautereau. The artist, born Alix Hava (1894-1989), was known professionally as Alix Aymé. She married Professor Paul de Fautereau-Vassel who, under the colonial regime, was based in Hanoi, where she taught drawing at the French Lycée. She then married French colonial officer General Georges Aymé. She was influential between the world wars, composing sensual portraits and captivating landscapes that fused exotic Southeast Asian styles with the spirit of Western, Paris-inspired modernism, sometimes compared to the work of Paul Gauguin (1848-1903). Exhibiting in Saigon, as well as Paris and Florence, she was commissioned by the Lao royal family to paint the reception hall's murals.

Her evocative, 'primitive' style pictures depict daily life in Luang Prabang as a rural idyll, starting from the left with the sun rising, continuing around the room and concluding on the right with the setting sun. The 19 canvases show the town's temples, in particular Wat Mai, in lush tropical settings, along with houses on stilts, local people, children, monks, markets, elephants with *howdahs*, and the flowing Mekong river with the magnificent mountains beyond. A palette of muted colours of ochres, earth browns, rust reds, purplish blues and greens, lends a romantic and paradisical atmosphere to the scenes.

The murals underwent a six week renovation project in 2004 by the French organisation Restaurateurs Sans Frontieres which mobilises conservators and restorers for heritage objects and monuments. They employed students from the Ecole de l'Art d'Avignon whose work revealed deterioration of 13 of the paintings. These were carefully treated and restored with materials brought from France and Thailand.

The Royal Palace viewed from Mount Phousi.

The Royal Palace with the central tower encased in scaffolding for restoration.

The palace, a cruciform layout set on a four-tiered platform, was designed by a French architect and constructed with the aid of Vietnamese workers. Walls and verandahs are of brick and white stucco, introduced by the French, while the red tiled roof sweeps down in the indigenous Lao style, ending with *cho faa,* flame-like tips. The ornate gable at the palace entrance depicts a golden three-headed elephant under a parasol, representing Indra's mount Erawan, and symbol of the former kingdom of *Lane Xang.* It is surrounded by fifteen golden *nagas.*

This is where the last King, Sisavangvong, was crowned in 1904. His son Savang Vatthana embellished it for a coronation that never took place.

The most important exhibit in the museum is the Pra Bang, the golden Buddha statue that gave its name to Luang Prabang, City of the Golden Buddha. A lavish new shrine, *chedi,* has been built to house the Pra Bang at the entrance to the museum grounds.

The Buddha statue is the most revered icon in Laos, worshipped as a talisman and a palladium, the safeguard and protector of the Kingdom. It was placed in a new shrine in the palace grounds in December 2013 with an elaborate ceremony attended by most of the city. Its symbolic value is what matters. Its removal by warring armies always signified defeat and its presence in the city is an assurance of peace and stability.

The statue is solid gold, weighs 43 kilograms, and stands 83 centimetres tall with hands raised in the *Abhayamudra* pose, 'giving protection' or 'dispelling fear'. Stylistically it would appear to date from around the 13th century. Its checkered history includes belonging to the king of Sri Lanka, King Phaya Sirichanta of Cambodia, and King Fa Ngum (r. 1353-73), founder of the 14th century Lao kingdom, *Lane Xang,* to whom it was presented by the King of Cambodia when he married a Cambodian princess. It was stolen several times by Siamese kings during succeeding centuries, and was eventually returned to Luang Prabang, to Wat Mai, then transferred to Wat Visoun.

On entering the museum, the first exhibit visitors see in the grandiose entrance hall is a gold painted lotus throne used for religious ceremonies by the Supreme Patriarch of the Buddhist Order. Beyond lies the king's reception room with busts of the last monarchs by French artists. The walls are covered with murals in a primitive style by French painter Alix de Fautereau, dating from 1930, depicting daily life in Luang Prabang as a rural idyll. The Queen's Reception Room has displays gifts from dignitaries around the world, ranging from tea sets from China, ivory from India, a boomerang from Australia and a piece of the moon from the Apollo 11 donated by Richard Nixon in 1973.

This tiny granite grey piece of the moon is encased in a transparent Lucite ball the size of a marble. It was one of the 'goodwill moon rocks', all hewn from mother rock 70017, collected in 1972 by Harrison Schmidt on the Apollo 11 mission, and then dedicated to the children of the world. Of the 382 kilograms of the moon rock gathered, a quarter of a kilogram was set aside for diplomatic purposes. Tiny fragments were given to 135 nations as gifts by President Nixon and then by President Ford. Each bore an inscription: "This Flag of Your Nation was Carried to the Moon and Back by Apollo 11." Today, many have gone missing, increasing the value of this one.

There are portraits of the last king and of Queen Kham Phoui, painted by Ilya Glazunov in 1967. The queen, dressed in a mauve silk embroidered outfit, her grey hair swept up into a traditional chignon on the side of her head, looks dignified but sad. On the left hand wall is one of the crown prince, Vongsavang. An artistic device of the portraits is that the eyes appear to follow one around the room.

The Pra Bang Buddha image is in the new shrine on the right after entering the palace grounds.

*** Highlight**

1. Solid gold stupa, just 59 cm high, encrusted with pearls, rubies, sapphires, amethysts and rose quartz crystal, bearing an image on each side of the Buddha in *bhumisparsa mudra*. Note the delicate golden flowers on stalks that extend outwards as if from a vase, above the Buddha.
2. Small crystal reclining Buddha, lying in *mahaparanirvana*, on a pedestal of beaten gold, possibly 15th century. The workmanship on this tiny yet luminous piece is remarkable.
3. Murals in King's Reception Room.
4. Queen's costumes, though few in number and modestly displayed, are of interest as examples of gold and silver thread embroidery.

The Throne Room is lavishly decorated. The bright red walls with Japanese glass mosaics, recall those of Wat Xieng Thong, which were created at the same time during the 1960s, by local artists including Thao Sing Kèo. There is a carved royal throne in the form of a *howdah,* a lightweight, highly refined platform designed to be raised by attendants on to the back of an elephant, adorned with a three-headed elephant insignia in gold, in which the Lao kings once rode in splendour. Also displayed are the brocade coronation robes for the Crown Prince, and cabinets containing the perfectly embroidered skirts, *sinh*, woven by the queen, featuring birds, butterflies, dragons and fish, in the Luang Prabang style, and adjacent shelves hold items such as delicate high-heeled black and gold lace shoes made in Nice, in France, for the queen.

Of particular interest is a glass case which displays a collection of exquisite 15th and 16th century gold and crystal Buddha images. Note the fine workmanship on even the smallest of these, some 36 having been retrieved from the That Makmo stupa in the town which was reportedly hit by lightning in the 17th century and then collapsed during a Chinese invasion of 1887. Other objects include those brought to earlier royal palaces to preserve them from theft. There are ceremonial daggers, one of which is small and encrusted with jewels, as well as eight golden betelnut cases, which were an essential accessory on social occasions when chewing betel was still in fashion.

The royal family's apartments are surprisingly modest for a royal abode, with polished teak floors and the original French furnishings. There is a grand empire-style bed in the king's bedroom, and a hand-cranked Victrola 'Talking Machine' from New Jersey, complete with old 78 rpm records of Pablo Casals. In the queen's bedroom is her silver brush and comb set. Crystal chandeliers, Sèvres porcelain dated 1889, with the royal insignia, as well as sedan chairs and a collection of Lao musical instruments, *don tri Lao deum,* comprising drums, cymbals, and bamboo flutes, decorate the sparsely furnished rooms.

Outside are the garages and stables. Here, visitors can see the old cars that belonged to the king. These include two white Lincoln Continentals, a Ford and a Citroën.

The gardens include a very old banyan tree, the magnificent avenue of palms leading to the palace, and a pond, surrounded by tropical flowers and trees.

A large statue of Sisavangvong to the left stands in front of the Winter Palace, constructed for the coronation of Savang Vatthana. This building is now used for dance performances and is called the Royal Ballet Theatre. Performances of the *Phra Lak Phra Lam* take place here four times a week, on Monday, Wednesday, Friday and Saturday at 17.30.

Solid gold stupa encrusted with precious stones. (Art et archéologie du Laos, Madeleine Giteau, Picard, 2001)

The Royal Ballet Theatre is on the left after entering the gate. (OC)

Performance of Phra Lak Phra Lam *at the Royal Ballet Theatre © Jean-Michel Gallet.*

Secular Architecture

Secular Architecture: Lao Vernacular and French Colonial Buildings

"I am in Luang Prabang, a wonder to the eyes. The city and its rivers and mountains incontestably the most beautiful spot in Laos." Auguste Pavie

Luang Prabang in the morning mist.

Luang Prabang's jewel-like identity arises from its combination of temples and domestic architecture – the sacred and the profane – and from its small, human scale. There is nothing monumental or overwhelming. Everything is subtle and aesthetically pleasing. While the more lavish ornamentation was reserved for temples, vernacular housing was embellished with simple but harmonious decoration. If you climb the 328 steps to the top of Mount Phousi and look down on Luang Prabang, the panorama has hardly changed since Pavie first saw it. Just three main streets, until recently completely traffic free, strung out with glittering temple roofs and golden spires, a white palace planted in the centre surrounded by ancient trees, and picturesque houses nestled amongst the exotic greenery. The sense of enchantment is enhanced by the unhurried pace of the place, set by strolling monks and children on bicycles, with fishermen descending into the river when the water is low to cast their nets. In the early morning light a barely perceptible grey mist veils everything, softening the contours, then gradually disperses with the sparkling sunlight to reveal the little town on a great river surrounded by majestic mountains.

Little wonder then that when the French arrived in the 19th century they felt they had stumbled into a remote garden of Eden. The French called Indochina *"Un pays de cocagne, un paradis terrestre,"* (a land of milk and honey, an earthly paradise). Luang Prabang was, in Norman Lewis's words in *A Dragon Apparent*, "a small, somnolent and sanctified Manhattan Island . . . the home-town of the siesta and the Ultima Thule of all French escapists in the Far East." Yet the French had come to colonise.

In his book *Orientalism,* Edward Said describes colonisation as "one of the most complex and delicate phenomena of social physiology." Although the aim of France was ostensibly profit and the enlargement of their territory, the colonisers brought a benevolent attitude and an artistic contribution, encompassing education and the indigenous acquisition of the French language as well as urban planning, a *mission civilisatrice.* "France distanced itself from acquisitive violent origins of empire," writes Dr. Nicola Cooper in *France in Indochina, Colonial Encounters.* France's approach to colonialism epitomised the humanitarian nature of French action abroad. "The notion of *mise en valeur* (improvement) lent itself readily as an example of an ethically based colonial goal with a beneficial outcome," she states, adding that Henri Mouhot's discovery of Luang Prabang and, before it,

Opposite: *View of Luang Prabang at the break of dawn.*

Overleaf: *The confluence of the Mekong and Nam Khan rivers.* (Courtesy *Luang Phabang: an architectural journey*)

The Opera House, Saigon. (RB)

Angkor in Cambodia, gave the French great prestige in artistic and cultural terms. These sites gave a glamour to Indochina, nourished by exotic writers such as Pierre Loti, and enhanced by colonial propaganda.

The French attitude is further examined in *Orientalism,* as Edward Said attributes France's quest to the historical context of the period. He believes that the expansionist fervor in France during the late 19th century was generated out of an explicit wish to compensate for the Prussian victory in 1870-1871 and, no less important the desire to match British imperial achievements. He claims that the latter was so powerful, borne of a long tradition of Anglo-French rivalry in the Orient, that France seemed literally haunted by Britain, anxious to catch up with all things connected with the Orient. When, in the late 1870s, the *Société Académique Indo-Chinoise* reformulated its goals, it found it important to "bring Indochina into the domain of Orientalism." Said concludes that it was in order to turn it into a 'French India.'

The result was that Indochina became *la perle de l'Extrême-Orient,* the pearl of the Far East. French architects and town planners, including Ernest Hébrard, Gustave Eiffel, creator of the Eiffel Tower, and Huyn de Verneville, rushed to its capitals, eager to use the cities as 'aesthetic laboratories,' displaying them as showcases of France's success and experimen-ting with the latest architectural ideas. In France, the 19th century was an era of unprecedented urban generation. With Baron Haussmann as Napoleon III's town planner, this was the period when Paris was laid out as a city of pomp and splendour. This was the era of the *belle époque*, when many of the greatest edifices were built, such as the Opera House, designed by Charles Garnier and inaugurated in 1875. This opulent building was copied in Hanoi and Saigon where similar French opera houses became the centrepieces of Asian capitals. If architecture is an expression of power, then the French propagated their superiority and hegemony via the cities of Indochina which, says Dr. Cooper, were made visibly French. The most significant examples are Hanoi, Saigon and Phnom Penh. In Vientiane and Luang Prabang the symbolism is there but more understated.

The French influence changed Laos gradually, making it a subtle blend of East and West. In Vientiane, the administrative but modest capital, they created wide tree lined boulevards for their villas and offices. A Catholic church and a School of Medicine were added. In Luang Prabang they introduced new building materials for their houses such as fired brick and ceramic roof tiles, hitherto reserved for temple building. The main attributes of their architecture were extended roof areas to protect against the hot sun and monsoon rains, with long, narrow

Opposite below: *The Colonial Department of Transport built during the French occupation.*

The Residence Superieure used to be the house of French officials in Luang Prabang.

windows, paned and shuttered, and double walls, one inside the other, so that cool breezes could flow through the building. In addition there were wrought iron balconies, stylish arcades, impressive entrances and elegant well-proportioned verandahs at the *piano nobile* level where occupants could lounge in the cool of evening. These were large, spacious houses for gracious living, dependent on a retinue of servants, cooks and gardeners.

Inside there would be high ceilings and fireplaces, for the winter months brought damp and mist, brick and wooden decorative details, lintels, cornices, capitals, ceramic tiles and elegant sculpted ornamentation reminiscent of the villas of Paris and Nice.

This *belle époque* architecture was harmonious, usually adhering to the geometry of the 'golden mean', the ratio used in classical buildings and Palladian architecture, whereby the height of a room is equal to its width, and the windows are a third of the whole space. These architectural ideas were cleverly, almost wittily, combined with Lao vernacular traditions and motifs, and a hybrid 'Indochinese style' was developed. As French influence increased, so Lao builders in turn incorporated aspects of French design into their work. The fusion of these two disparate cultures created a unique style. The legacy is still visible today in many parts of Laos, especially in Luang Prabang, as well as in Cambodia and Vietnam.

Top: *Colonial house.*
Above: *Old French house.*
Below: *Lao wooden house.*

Although many buildings are inevitably dilapidated and neglected as a result of war and poverty, others have been restored by a new generation of French visitors, this time entrepreneurs and hoteliers, who have returned with nostalgia to their beloved *Indochine.*

To protect these historic buildings, UNESCO, when making Luang Prabang a World Heritage Site in 1993, included them all, as the designation covered the entire town. Their specialised architects, under the aegis of Francis Engelmann, have now produced a definitive map showing every one of the 443 protected civil buildings as well as the 177 sacred structures that comprise 33 monasteries, making a total of 620 edifices.

But Luang Prabang is a living city rather than a museum. Its population of about 12,000 people, with some 35,000 in the whole district, continue to live and work here. However, being an increasingly popular site of 'heritage tourism' is leading to a change in these demographics as more Luang Prabang residents lease out their properties to hotel developers and move elsewhere. While the preservation of these fragile structures is vital, renovation progresses only when funding can be found for domestic buildings.

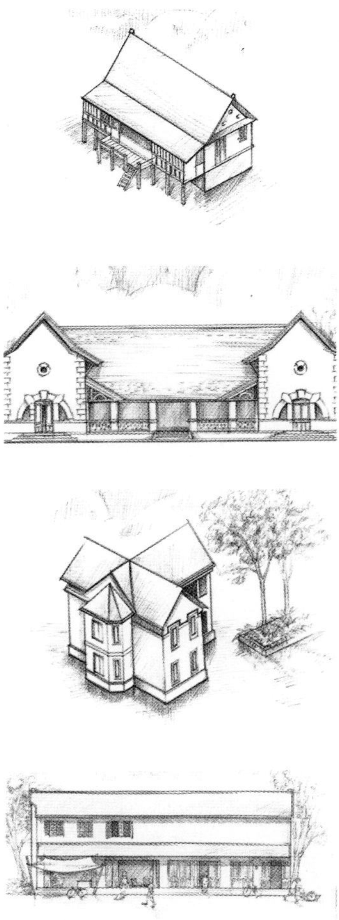

Four different types of buildings categorised by UNESCO.

In its study of the town's secular architecture, UNESCO has identified five specific indigenous styles in Luang Prabang and classified them as: simple roof or double roof; simple roof with verandah; simple roof with verandah and a kitchen that is perpendicular to the building; compartment house; compartment building; finally, colonial architecture. These wooden buildings are not very old, as the town was attacked several times during the 19th century and many of the traditional houses disappeared, so many date from the early 20th century.

The traditional Lao house is made of tropical hardwood or bamboo, built on stilts. The roof of the Lao stilted house has high pitched gables or is hipped (the angle formed where two sloping sides of a roof meet) with extended eaves to prevent leaking. The assembled structure, decorated with intricately carved fretwork and delicate floral or geometric patterns, is covered with terracotta tiles or palm leaves. The transom, above the door, is usually ornately carved. Religious scriptures encourage house-holders to have their door frame in carved wood to signify the threshold and to welcome visitors. Many typical houses will have a verandah projecting in front, providing ventilation for the rooms. These have decoratively carved balustrades and sometimes a wooden trellis. The kitchen is always apart from the living area, a building usually attached on one side, so that the preparation of food is a separate activity from the rest of domestic life.

Walls and partitions may be of woven bamboo, in herringbone style, crisscrossed or plaited. Some houses are made entirely of bamboo, which is a less expensive option than wood. Bamboo homes tended, therefore, to belong to the poorer section of the population. The entire structure of the house – can be constructed with bamboo as it is so strong and waterproof. According to Bounthieng Siripapthanh, in *Laos and Ethnic Minority Cultures,*

Traditional houses built of wood and raised on stilts. The verandah of such houses are an important area for relaxing and receiving visitors.

House with prayer flag.

Top left: *Fret-work balcony on a traditional Lao house.*

Laos has some 700 species of bamboo. Many tools, baskets, domestic utensils and boats and rafts are also made from this versatile plant.

Raising a house on stilts is eminently practical. It affords ventilation in the heat and protection from flooding in the monsoon season and from animals and insects. The area underneath provides a sheltered area for cooking, storage and family activities. The tendency for living in houses on stilts is supposedly drawn from historical 16th century Lao texts, *Nithan Khun Burôm,* which record that Khun Borom, son of the King of the higher divinities, *Then,* descended to earth to become the king of the world. Khun Lo, one of his seven children, was given the Kingdom of Luang Prabang. It is said that in the demarcation of Lao and Vietnamese kingdoms, Khun Lo could identify his people by their stilt dwellings. This legend evolved into fact when negotiations for a frontier between Lane Xang and Annam occurred in the 17th century. It was agreed that those people occupying stilted houses would owe allegiance to the Kingdom of Lane Xang, whereas those living at ground level would owe allegiance to the Dai Viet of Annam. Housing, therefore, is fundamental to national identity as well as to social formation.

A house with woven bamboo walls.

Local aesthetic preferences govern the design of a house as much as architectural principles and the structures are an integral part of the community, embodying superstitious beliefs and social standing. Religious and secular architecture overlap and a similar style can be used to house Buddhist monks or lay people. An altar with family relics and a Buddha image is present in every home.

The Lao believe that their lives are ruled by natural and supernatural forces, and many ancient beliefs are incorporated into the house.

An earlier phase of the building of Pavie's house. He stands on the porch of his house dressed in white (at the centre of the picture).

The siting of a house is an important act and it is always oriented auspiciously, based on ancestral lore ritually handed down, usually towards water. The process for building is also connected to local beliefs and subsequently associated with certain rites and ceremonies. An astrologer would be consulted to prevent any disturbance of the spirit guardians which inhabit the land, and a propitious period would be chosen for felling trees and preparing the frame of the house. Suitable materials have to be used for the construction, with candles, incense and chanting monks attending each stage. Prayers are said at the beginning and at the end of construction, and prior to occupation the owner will have the house blessed by the monks who bring flowers and holy water. If a house changes hands, again a prayer ceremony ensues so that the spirits of the house are appeased, and more prayers will welcome a new owner.

The bedroom is arranged so that a sleeping person, in accordance with ancient beliefs, points their head towards the south. One rule stipulates that the sleeping person should be perpendicular to the line of the roof of the house which, in turn, had to be parallel with the river. The head of the sleeper has to be placed against the partition that is opposite the point from where the air is circulated around the room. The feet can never be over the head of anyone else sleeping. Sleeping with the head towards the west is taboo, as the setting sun symbolises death.

Auspicious trees are planted around the house and the whole is a harmonious amalgam of beliefs, practicality and aesthetics.

Half-cement half-wood house. Built after the arrival of the French.

Small spirit houses are found in the grounds of most Lao homes, a miniature structure resembling a house, often very simple, and raised on a pole. These are believed to contain the spiritual guardian, *phi,* of the home, and are a link with earlier animistic beliefs. Offerings of rice, flowers and incense are brought to the spirit house every day.

While some of these wooden houses are in a ruinous state, brick and stucco homes, like the sacred structures, are regularly repainted as the torrential rainy season tends to wash off much of the colour and spoil the whitewash. So every dry season sees a repainting of many buildings. Traditionally, the colonial buildings were whitewashed and the shutters painted blue.

The changing face of Luang Prabang; this row of traditional shop houses was transformed into cafes in 2012.

With French building came the introduction of lime mortar, made with as many as 30 ingredients, including sandstone, sugar cane, boiled buffalo skin, which makes good glue, tree juice, water, bananas lime which gives strength and powdered limestone. Lime (a concentration of calcium compounds) allows vapour to pass through, and is better adapted to the climate. Cement is easy to use but only as a short term solution, and although it has been adopted in Luang Prabang, it is not the optimum material for conservation.

Another typical form of housing found throughout Southeast Asia as well as in Laos are the old Chinese shophouses. These are a combination of both commercial and residential premises, with the shop on the ground floor while above are the living quarters. At street level the building has an extended awning or arcade, a covered passageway called the 'five foot way', originally a feature of British colonial cities in Asia, such as Singapore. There are many of these along the main road in Luang Prabang and of late they have been transformed into guesthouses, coffeeshops and bakeries, catering for tourists. Most of these establishments have kept the original interiors, with tables and chairs spilling out in to the area beneath the arcade, and adding Lao woven materials and red check tablecloths to complete the welcoming effect.

A small selection of the many Lao and French houses in Luang Prabang appear on the following pages.

Part of a row of Chinese-style shophouses has been turned into a shop and cafe.

Location: Sakkarine Road, Ban Wat Nong
Date: 1898
Style: Lao Vernacular
Tel: (+856-71) 253-888
Website: www.3nagas.com

Auberge Three Nagas (Originally the Lamache House)

This house is made from local hardwood with whitewashed walls and wooden beams and three wooden double doorways, with an overhanging wooden terrace supported by simple rectangular wood columns. Inside there is a central wooden staircase, and red tiled floors. The rooms upstairs have high ceilings under the red tiled roof, with dark wood beams and polished wood floors. It has been sympathetically restored and is now a charming boutique hotel where guests can bask in a Lao atmosphere. Large ceiling fans add to the effect, and, being traditional, are a more appropriate cooling system than air conditioning.

The entrance to 3 Nagas Hotel.

Built by a Mr Lamache, it was initially used to hold meetings by the officials of the Royal Court. A few decades later, his grand-children opened an ice-cream shop. Their product became so popular in Luang Prabang that they were appointed as the official Royal Court ice-cream supplier. During recent restoration work, French-Canadian architect Pascal Trahan, who has leased and renovated the building, came across three bottles still filled with the essence extracts for the ice-cream flavours. These are sometimes displayed in the main lobby.

The house was restored using traditional techniques and with respect to the fundamental structure. Most of the woodwork, floors, furniture and a modern staircase are made with a local wood called *May Pow,* originally used in the construction of boats.

The final result is an intimate atmosphere inspired by tradition with all the modern comforts and facilities.

École de la Santé Publique

Location: Chao Fa Ngum Road
Date: 20th century
Style: French colonial

A simple French colonial one-storey low whitewashed building with a projecting roof supported by six rectangular columns and blue painted shuttered long windows with semicircular tops.

The View Pavilion

Location: Sakkarine Road
Date: 1935
Style: French Colonial

This French colonial-styled house was built in 1935. The land had belonged to a Mrs Tanh, who had a beautiful daughter, Onh. Onh married a Frenchman, Monsieur Marcheau, a veterinary doctor, whose office at that time was in the Villa Xiengkeo. Her mother gave them the land as a wedding present, and the house was then built by French architects.

The couple had two daughters, and eventually they and their father went to France. Onh remarried and had a son, Angkham, and he inherited the house which he subsequently sold.

The white stucco two storey house with an external wooden staircases and a wraparound wooden balcony is a fine example of a French house with Lao architectural detail. The two sides of the house have four columns each. These support a simple wooden terrace all around the first floor, creating a shaded ground floor area. The positioning of the first floor corresponds to the perfect symmetry of the 'golden mean,' whereby the height of the ground floor is taller than the first floor, so that the balcony or terrace is closer to the roof than the ground.

The View Pavilion.

Sala Prabang

Location: Oun Kham Road, Ban Xieng Mouane
Date: 1890
Style: Lao traditional secular
Tel: (+856 71) 252-460
Website: www.salalao.com

Facing the river, this is now a boutique style hotel. It is a traditional 19th century wooden house, with its terrace covered with a profusion of purple and red bougainvillea. With a single pitched roof and four supporting columns in the front, it has a first floor terrace with attractive carved balustrades, in two styles, shuttered windows and a spacious ground floor porch area with four steps up from the road.

In the 1940s it belonged to the Prime Minister of Laos, Phaya Kamao, and the current owner has a photograph of himself with Prince Phetsarath. It was converted into a boutique hotel and the interior was sensitively restored by architect Sinlasone Soumpholphakdy, with an abundance of local wood, original flooring and simple whitewashed walls, maintaining a period atmosphere. There is a flower filled courtyard at the back.

The two storey Sala Prabang hotel looks out on to the Mekong.

Location: Sakharine Road, Ban Wat Nong
Date: 1903
Style: Lao Vernacular
Tel: (+856-71) 252-079
Website: www.3nagas.com

Khamboua House

Opposite the Three Nagas, this mansion, with its traditional features of Lao architecture such as a single pitched roof, verandah and perpendicular kitchen, is one of the finest in this World Heritage Site. Built in 1903 by one of the counsellors to King Sisavangvong, it uses teak and rosewood, for the structure and flooring, and traditional *torchis* walls, which is lime screed on a bamboo structure.

According to the Venerable Patriarch of Wat Sene, a member of the family which owns the building, all the major pieces of the wooden framework were brought on site using elephants across the Nam Khan river. Located in the centre of the historic town, it is the only house with a 500 square metre garden backing on to the river.

A colonial building next to Khamboua house highlights the different architectural styles.

Now a part of the Three Nagas hotel, Khamboua House was built in traditional Lao style.

Location: Souvannakham-phong Road, 150 metres from Wat Xieng Thong
Date: 1904
Style: French colonial mansion
Tel: (+856 71) 212-100
Email: calaoinn@laotel.com

Auberge Calao

This renovated two-storey mansion dating from 1904, with a steep roof and five arched balconies, offers a direct view on to the Mekong river. It is painted the traditional pale yellow, popular throughout Indochina, with stucco architectural details attractively picked out in white. Wrought iron gates open up to steep steps rising up from the street, with two sets of terraces shaded by umbrellas. The façade is composed of a ground floor with arcades harmoniously balanced by the enclosed terraces above with their five semicircular arches interspersed with white low relief columns.

Lane Xang Travel and Guesthouse, a half-timbered house.

Location: Chao Sisouphan Road, opposite Wat Visoun
Date: Early 20th century
Style: Lao French wood and stucco on stilts
Tel: (+856-71) 212-794

Lane Xang Travel and Guesthouse

A blend of Lao wooden architecture and French stucco, on white stucco stilts, this L-shaped building on stilts has a pitched roof, a verandah in the middle, wooden shutters and graceful proportions. The wooden structure is visible with beams interspersed with daub walls.

UNESCO: La Maison du Patrimoine

Location: Sakharine Road
Date: 1932
Style: French colonial

This is the former French Customs House, built in 1932, close to Wat Xieng Thong and Wat Pak Khan, at the tip of Luang Prabang. With its pitched roof and extended eaves, perfect for protecting the building in heavy rain. It has an exterior, plain staircase at the front, leading to the first floor. The front façade has a front two storey square projection, with the front door below, with a simple narrow rectangular shuttered window on either side, and a room above where the floor length French style windows open up completely, giving a graceful aspect to the whole.

It is the office of the conservation and development advisory service for the citizens of Luang Prabang, part of the service of the Provincial Authorities. This office reports to the Local Provincial Committee for the Protection and Development of Cultural and Natural Heritage and is part of the Safeguarding and Development Plan of Luang Prabang, under the aegis of UNESCO.

The UNESCO building is a colonial house in pale pink with blue shutters.

Location: Alley off Sakkarine Road behind Wat Xieng Mouane
Date: Early 20th century
Style: Traditional Lao vernacular

Villa Xieng Mouane

Villa Xieng Mouane, now referred to as the Heritage House, a traditional Lao wooden house renovated in 1997.

An admirable old house belonging to Madame Phoupha, in an alley that has now been paved with bricks. The bosky setting is especially romantic, with tall coconut palms and spindley sugar palms bringing shade to this spacious traditional Lao house. It is raised on short, sturdy rectangular stilts, five to each side, with a two tiered roof, the main one covering the central structure and the subsidiary one over the projecting front verandah. The front wall of the verandah is wood and the sides are daub. A wooden staircase leads first to a small open landing that in turn leads on to the enclosed verandah.

From within, the visitor steps through a shuttered doorway into the main living area. Looking up, the roof beams are visible from the inside and there are well maintained polished wood floors. On the side of the house there are two long windows with louvred doors. At times, *Baci* ceremonies for visitors have been performed here.

Location: Ban Xieng Mouane
Date: 1904
Style: Lao

Puang Champa Cultural House

Hidden down a small alley The Little House, as it is called, is a wooden house on stilts and is now run under the auspices of the Lao Heritage Foundation as a small museum and well worth a visit. Built in 1904 and renovated in 2005, Puang Champa Cultural House was created to teach traditional crafts such as gold thread embroidery, ceremonial flower arranging, dance, literature and instrument making. It is filled with antiques such as Buddha images, masks and crowns worn by dancers in productions of the *Phra Lak Phra Lam* and a collection of more than a hundred historic Lao textiles. These were accumulated by antique collecter Mr Keomontree Duangbupha who travelled in the northern parts of Laos where many traditional silkweaving patterns and styles had once flourished among the Tai Deang, Lue and Lao ethnic communities. He realised that this rich heritage was in danger of being lost and was determined to preserve textile designs for future weavers.

COLONIAL HOUSE

Location: Souvannakamphong Road
Date: 1920s
Style: French Colonial

This two-storey whitewashed French colonial building has a central doorway at the *piano nobile* level, with white louvre shutters and two shuttered windows on either side. The façade decoration of rectangular low-relief carved pillars, interspersed with carved hemispherical cornices decorated with Lao imagery of sunbursts, flowers and birds at the centre, add elegance to this simple building. A rather grand double staircase leading to the front door in brick with carved balustrades is based on the traditional staircases that ascend to most wooden houses. The abundant tropical greenery of the garden, offset by a wrought iron gate and French white picket fence with square columns, and a newel post in the form of a lotus, create a delightful Lao-French, East-West fusion to this privately owned villa.

COLONIAL HOUSE

Location: Setthathirat corner of Sam Saentai Road
Date: Early 20th century
Style: French Colonial

An imposing tall, spacious French colonial building of two storeys in a *belle époque* style, now converted into a restaurant. It has long slender windows with blue shutters and a protruding front bay.

Location: Sakkarine Road, Ban Wat Nong
Date: 1890s
Style: French colonial villa
Tel: (+856-71) 212-267
Website: www.villasantihotel.com

Top: *Villa Santi is in colonial style. It is similar to Calao Inn except for its roof that has a tiny dormer window in the middle.*

VILLA SANTI

This colonial mansion, built in the 1890s, belonged to the royal family and is a now a hotel run by Santi Inthavong, husband of Princess Mahnilee, grand-daughter of Savang Vatthana. Her mother Princess Mahnilee was pregnant with her seventh child in 1975 and did not depart with the rest of the family but remained in Luang Prabang. It was one of the first hotels to open in Luang Prabang after the country opened up again to tourism, and was called Villa de la Princess, and then the Villa Santi.

Villa Santi has a covered terrace on the *piano nobile* with five semicircular arcades on columns, with carved balustrades, resem-bling a portico and loggia of a classical building. The pitched roof has a tiny dormer window in the front with small Lao finials. The roof has a Lao style metal decoration on the top similar to a *cho faa*. Full length French windows with Lao style carved transoms above each one open out on to the terrace from a long dining room with polished wood floors. On the ground floor there is a main doorway with louvred doors that open right back with a semicircular carved transom above, and additional doorways on either side.

School of Fine Arts, a half-timbered building. Note the beautiful carved decorations on the roof.

Saynamkhan Guesthouse

This elegant two-storey French colonial house, now a guesthouse, is on a corner facing the Nam Khan river. With four windows along the side street, it has a window and front entrance on the corner, with nine shuttered windows facing the river, and a terrace with long French windows on the ground floor. The pitched roof is Lao influenced. At night the ground floor is lit with lanterns.

Location: King Kitsarath Road, Ban Wat Sene
Date: early 20th century
Style: French colonial
Tel: (+856-71) 212-976
Website: www.saynamkhanhotel-luangprabang.com

Resident Superieure's House

Now the Bureau de l'Administration Provincale de Luang Prabang, this imposing two-storey mansion was the residence of the French Resident Superieure in colonial times.

It has a projecting central square verandah on the *piano nobile,* over the front door below, and open at the sides to allow cool breezes to flow freely. The *piano nobile* has an open area with wooden blinds along its entire length, under the pitched roof, also permitting the air to circulate around the building. On the ground floor, the doorway is flanked by three windows with semicircular tops and a smaller square window, all with blue shutters. Four steps lead up to the main, square pillared entrance.

Location: Chao Fa Ngum Road
Date: 19th century
Style: French colonial villa

Location: Chao Fa Ngum Road, Ban That Luang
Date: 1962
Style: French colonial mansion
Tel: (+856-71) 254-609
Website: www.coloursofangsana.com

Maison Souvannaphoum

This stylish French colonial mansion with Lao motifs belonged to Prince Souvannaphouma (1901-1984), half brother of Souvannouvong and of Phetsarath, when he was Prime Minister. It has been restored and redeveloped as a hotel with new buildings in the garden, discreetly co-ordinated. On the main building, painted brilliant white, a projecting verandah with four columns creates an impressive shaded entrance for the main doorway. The roof is typically Lao in style with a decorative roof edging with pointed finials. It has undergone several renovations.

Location: Chao Sisouphan Road. Adjacent to Lane Xang Travel and Guesthouse
Date: Early 20th century
Style: French/Lao wooden

Red Cross Building

This wooden house on stilts is a blend of Lao and French, with visible wood beams and daub, painted white and blue.

Satri House

Location: Photthisarath Road, Ban That Luang
Date: 1900
Style: French colonial villa
Tel: (+856-71) 253-491-2
Fax: (+856 71) 253-418
Website: http://www.satrihouse.com

A French colonial two-storey villa which has been converted into a stylish boutique hotel. Satri House was built in 1900 by *Oupahat* Boun Khong and his 11th wife, the parents of Prince Souvannouvong the 'Red Prince'. Souvannouvong lived here until the age of 11 years old. The house remained in the possession of relatives of the family until 1998 when they sold it to a local financier. It was purchased by 2001 by Lamphoune Voravongsa and transformed into a hotel.

It has a pitched tiled roof and whitewashed stucco walls with French mouldings. It has a *belle époque* feel with four long elegant windows on the first floor, all with polished brown shutters, and on the ground floor a front entrance resembling French windows, with four steps and brown louvre wooden shutters, flanked by two windows on one side and one on the other. On the side of the house are further windows, embellished with Lao carved balustrades.

The interior has been artistically decorated with great panache by Lamphoune Voravongas with Lao silks and antique furniture.

Yellow House

Location: Phone Heuang Road
Date: 1900s
Style: Lao/French

This pretty, traditional wooden house painted chrome yellow, hence its name, is next to Wat Xieng Thong on one side and the former residence of the King on the other (now demolished, regrettably). It formed part of a 'royal compound' of residences around the temple and belonged to a member of the royal family. The ground floor is of brick and stucco, painted yellow, while the upper floor is traditional wood with a verandah that is enclosed by a wood screen. It has a double pitched roof and steps leading up to the front door.

During the 1970s the house fell into disrepair and in 2002 was acquired by a new owner. With the technical assistance of UNESCO it was carefully restored to its former appearance with every architectural and historic detail recreated.

Opposite: *The half timbered Red Cross building used to be called Ban Visoun. It was restored to its present state in 1994.* (© The Yellow House Photo Sia Lee)

Location: Phone Heuang Road, near Elephant Blanc restaurant
Date: 1925
Style: Lao/French

Colonial Houses

Maison Seng Tiane Phanith is one of the largest colonial houses of Luang Prabang, mixing French influences with some local and Chinese characteristics. It was built in 1925 by a rich Chinese merchant who married a Lao woman. His grand-daughter, who lives in Vientiane, still owns the house. The ground floor is brick and stucco, whitewashed, with grey shuttered doors and windows. The first floor is wood, with an attractive wooden verandah with typical carved balustrades. The roof is tiled with Lao motifs.

A brick and wooden house.

Half-brick half-wooden house with carved balcony.

Location: Ban That Luang
Date: 1900s
Style: French Colonial

Le Pavillon de Jade

A small but pretty two-storey French colonial house painted pale pink. Although just one room wide, the proportions are pleasing and elegant. It has a first floor wood verandah, painted green, with an exterior wooden staircase rising from the ground floor, a feature of French colonial architecture. It has been a silk boutique since 2001 with a workshop at the back with weavers from Ban Phanom weaving village. They obtain silk from silk worms fed on banana and manioc leaves. These produce a raw silk that is thicker and, when hand spun, is more like a textured wool, making it unique among Lao textiles.

XIENGKEO MANSION (Prince Phetsarath's former house)

Location: Ban Xiengkeo, Khet Sangkalok. Overlooking Mekong river, 4 kilometres from the town centre
Date: 1920s
Style: French Colonial Mansion
Tel: (+856-71) 253-851-7
Website: www.grandluangprabang.com

Now The Grand Luang Prabang, Xiengkeo Mansion has an incomparable location overlooking the Mekong river, and is an especially fine example of French colonial style architecture in an idyllic tropical setting. Built in the 1920s, it belonged to a Frenchman, possibly an officer or a businessman, from whom it was bought by Prince Phetsarath (1890-1959), the revered nationalist and 'iron man' of Laos. He renovated it and lived in it for only a short period, a few years before he died.

If ever a building adhered to the classical notion of architectural symmetry relating to the space around it, this is it. Its rural setting overlooking the river must have been conceived with every auspicious detail in place. The original structure is a cruciform shape, with a wide, arcaded entrance with two pillars, square below and then rounded, supporting a first floor teak wood verandah with louvre doors, like plantation shutters, that fold open to transform it into an open air space.

Two storeys high, it has a pitched tiled roof with extended eaves, supported by rounded wooden beams, perfect for protecting the sides of the house during the heavy monsoon rains. Long, elegant wooden shuttered windows punctuate each wall, with decorative cornicing above in two rows, and finishing, under the eaves, with decorative tiles. The architect, by applying the classical measurements to the proportions of the villa made the ground floor taller than the first.

A small room on the first floor is a veritable shrine to the prince, with his photo and an altar with flowers. He is revered by the Laotions, who invest him with almost supernatural qualities and bring offerings on the anniversay of his death.

Exterior walls with shuttered windows give way to interior walls with wide openings, a feature of tropical architecture which allowed the flow of cool breezes. The ground floor has a low, simple semicircular fireplace for early mornings in Luang Prabang are cool, and a back staircase for staff. The *piano nobile* has a main room with art-deco style painted cornices, leading to the

Prince Phetsarath's shrine in Xiengkeo Mansion (below).

The elegant residence of Prince Phetsarath.

shuttered verandah, with black and white floor tiles. In the evening or early morning these louvre shutters would have been folded back to reveal the stunning panorama of the river and mountains at a broad bend in the Mekong river, upstream from Luang Prabang.

The house has classically proportioned rooms which are light and airy and would have been a haven of elegance when furnished traditionally and decorated with textiles. Although austere, they are eminently practical for the tropical climate, as breezes would have circulated around the open rooms. The prince entertained in the main room and on the verandah. It is easy to imagine him with friends, or alone in contemplation, in the setting that is incomparably romantic, with brilliantly clear night skies where he must have indulged his interest in astronomy. Tragically, these skies would soon be filled with fighter jets as the shadow of war fell across Laos. This refined way of life was about to vanish forever.

The painted cornice in art deco style. (OC)

After the Pathet Lao seized power in 1975 it was left empty. Although it has been extensively restored and redecorated, there are no fixtures and fittings, apart from electric ceiling fans and the simple black and white floor tiles, and there is not even a bathroom. Nevertheless, it has a special atmosphere.

Below: *The mansion at night. Even though guests cannot stay in this building, one can enjoy this spectacular sight.*

The Traditional Arts and Ethnology Centre Luang Prabang

Location: Behind Dara Market at foot of Mount Phousi
Date: 1920s
Style: Traditional Lao House
Website: http://www.taeclaos.org
Tel: +856 (0) 71 253 364

The Traditional Arts and Ethnology Centre is the first of its kind in the former royal capital to celebrate and preserve the diversity and creativity of the country's ethnic minorities. This traditional Lao house was originally built for a colonial judge during the 1920s. A Category One listed heritage building it has had many uses including military court and private residence.

The TAEC, an independent, non-profit institution, opened as a resource centre and museum in 2007 after undergoing a six month restoration. Maintaining its original fireplaces and layout, it now houses more than 300 cultural artefacts.

The collection enhances understanding of Laos' wealth of ethnic culture. Some 49 different ethnic minorities exist within a population of 6.8 million people of whom only 52% are ethnic Lao.

Regular exhibitions and permanent displays highlight different aspects of ethnic culture, such as Hmong weddings and celebrations of New Year, weaving styles of the Khmu, the dyeing techniques of the Tai Dam and woven bamboo objects of the Akha ethnic minorities. On view are exuberantly coloured hand-dyed cotton and silk costumes, some with tightly pleated skirts, high turbans, shimmering head-dresses and finely wrought silver jewellery, as well as domestic utensils and recreations of interiors of homes. The museum attracts local and foreign visitors and scholars. Their gift shop, operating on fairtrade principles, sells woven pieces, art objects and books.

Akha headdress.

Traditional Arts and Ethnology historic house built 1920s.

Typical costume of ethnic minorities.

Vientiane and Beyond

Vientiane
Wat Phra That Luang
Wat Sisaket
Wat Ho Phra Kaeo
Wat Si Muang
Wat Ong Teu
Patuxai
Lao Textiles Gallery
Lao Presidential Palace
Lao National Museum
Vang Vieng
Luang Namtha
Muang Sing
The Plain of Jars
Wat Phu
Paksé
Huei Thamo

SMOKE-FREE MUSEUM

VIENTIANE

Wat Phra That Luang by Louis Delaporte.

Vientiane, located on a bend in the Mekong River overlooking Thailand, was a quiet and modest capital but is gradually becoming a busier city. Originally called Vieng Chan, City of the Moon, it dates back to the 10th century and may have been a Khmer settlement during the expansion of the Angkorian empire between the 9th and 15th centuries.

In 1354 King Fa Ngum (r. 1353-73) founded the kingdom of Lane Xang, making Vientiane an administrative centre. Under King Photthisarat, (r. 1520-47), it became a religious centre and a focus for trade as well. King Setthathirat (r. 1548-71), officially established it as the capital of Lane Xang in 1563 and many Buddhist temples were built. It became a vassal of Siam in 1778 during the reign of King (Chao) Inthavong. King Anou Vong succeeded his brother Inthavong to the throne in 1805 and built Wat Sisaket. He invaded Siam and captured Korat but the Siamese, under General Sing Singhaseni, defeated him after his army was pursued back to Vientiane. King Rama III of Siam then ordered the sacking of Vientiane in 1827 which, apart from Wat Sisaket, was completely destroyed. Anou Vong was captured and imprisoned by the Siamese, kept in an iron cage until his death in 1829, aged 62.

When Francis Garnier arrived in 1867 with the Mekong Exploration Team, led by Doudart de Lagreé, he found only the dusty ruins of a deserted city overgrown by tropical vegetation.

Old colonial house Vientiane.

Under the French colonial regime, from 1893, the city became the capital of the French protectorate of Laos and was restored, including Wat That Luang, Wat Sisaket and Wat Ho Phra Kaeo. Governor-General Paul Doumer signed a decree in 1900 dividing the province into four *muang*, states, Vientiane, Borikan, Patchoum, Tourakom. French town planners laid out several wide boulevards in a geometrical street plan, lined with handsome colonial villas and shady tropical trees, adding a governer's residence, as well as a colonial style *Ecole de Medicine* (Medical School) and a Catholic Church, the *Sacre-Coeur*, built in 1928. Unlike Luang Prabang, these are not protected as cultural heritage by UNESCO. Some have survived, such as the attractive villas that now comprise the French Embassy, while unfortunately others have not.

During the turbulent war years of 1960s and 1970s, Vientiane became a refuge for journalists, secret agents and American soldiers from the Vietnam war. Among others, Hunter Thompson, inventor of gonzo journalism, retreated to Vientiane's Lane Xang Hotel to write dispatches after escaping from Saigon. The city became notorious for its louche bars and opium dens. All this faded after the Communist Pathet Lao victory in 1975 as it came under Soviet rule.

Opposite: *Wat Ho Phra Kaeo Doorway.*

Chao Anou Vong.

Currently Vientiane is undergoing a revival with new hotels and conference centres. There is a new riverfront promenade extending the full length of Fa Ngum Road and beyond, where one can stroll and bicycle to enjoy river views and visit colourful night markets that have sprung up. In 2010, at the 450th Anniversary celebrations of the capital, the government created the Chao Anou Vong Park, with a large bronze statue of the revered king.

Wat Phra That Luang

Location: Thanon That Luang
Date: 1566

The most revered temple in Laos and a focus for New Year celebrations, it is situated at the top of a hill three kilometres northeast of the city centre. With its golden, sinuously shaped spire shimmeringe at sunset it looks impressive from afar. However, close up it proves to be a concrete reproduction whose gilding is yellow paintwork. The symbolic square shape of the temple and central spire suggest the influence of Khmer sacred architecture. A stupa was built here, according to legend, in the 3rd century, to house a relic of the Buddha, a piece of his breast bone, reputedly brought by emissaries of the Mauryan Emperor Asoka. According to an inscription, King Setthathirat constructed a temple on the site in 1566 when he moved the capital here from Luang Prabang. A statue of him sits in front, in traditional costume, glittering in the evening sun along with the spire. In succeeding centuries the temple was destroyed by the Siamese and then the Chinese Ho in the late 19th century. Early in the 19th century, King Anou Vong (1805-1828) restored it, adding a cloister and pavilion. During the French colonial regime it was successfully reconstructed by French scholars of Angkor.

In the cloister there are several statues including one seated in the *dhyana mudra* position of meditation thought to be the thought to be the Khmer King Jayavarman VII (r. 1181-1220).

King Setthathirat.

Wat Sisaket

Location: Thanon Setthathirat
Date: 1818
Open: 8-12 and 1- 4 daily

This serene *wat* is a haven of peace in an increasingly busy city. Although dating only from 1818, it is the oldest *wat* in Vientiane and is a museum of sacred art. It was built for King Anou Vong (1805-1828) and escaped the destruction of the Siamese 1827 invasion. Restoration took place under the École Française d'Extrême Orient which brought Lao sculptors to renovate the wood carving and artisans from the School of Fine Arts in Phnom Penh, Cambodia.

Wat Sisaket cloisters.

It has a significant architectural feature in the form of cloisters. Rare in Lao *wats*, they are set in a square, a symbol of the absolute in Hindu sacred architecture, with the *sim* in the centre. The cloisters create an enclosed space, isolated from the rest of the outside world, a refuge for meditation, and are filled with 2,052 Buddha images. These are cast in bronze or carved in wood, with many more miniature images in pairs in symmetrical niches. Many Buddha statues were brought here for safekeeping. They are predominantly in the *bhumisparsa mudra*, with a few in the standing Calling For Rain *mudra*. Lining the cloister, they radiate serenity. Although unlabelled, some are, however, numbered. Notable is a Buddha Maravijaya – Triumphing over the Demon Mara in *bhumisparsa mudra* – number 28 that dates from 1491, according to an inscription. The head was re-attached to the torso in an unfortunate way that accentuates its strange countenance. Note the stylised ears like small leaves and the large twisted curls of hair.

There is a small copy of the Pra Bang Buddha in Luang Prabang (*see page 167*).

The *sim*, with its five-tiered roof, was restored by the French. Inside are faded murals and larger images of the Buddha. Notable is a sacred altar screen dating from 1820 carved and lacquered, with an immense *naga,* representing the cosmic ocean.

Wat Sisaket main sim.

Location: Thanon Setthathirat
Date: 1565, rebuilt 1936

Wat Ho Phra Kaeo

Wat Ho Phra Kaeo front view.

This *wat* is a replica of the original royal temple built in 1565 by King Setthathirat to venerate the Emerald Buddha, the Phra Kaeo, which was removed by the Siamese in 1779 by General Chakri, the future King Rama I, when he ransacked the city. The Buddha, which is made of jadeite rather than emerald, was taken to Bangkok where it has remained. Although damaged, the *wat* survived but was subsequently destroyed in 1827 by another Siamese invasion. It was then rebuilt, in concrete, between 1936-1942 during the French colonial regime under the aegis of Henri Parmentier of the École Française d'Extrême Orient, following original plans, and supervised by the artistic Prince Souvannaphouma (1901-1984) who would become Prime Minister in 1956 (*see page 24*). It is now a museum, surrounded by well tended gardens. There is a stone jar from the Plain of Jars exhibited in the far corner.

The *wat* has a sweeping three tiered roof and is surrounded by a raised gallery with six hexagonal columns, stuccoed and gilded, at the eastern entrance and seven along the north and south sides, with six at the rear western end. Along the galleries of the *sim* is an outstanding collection of bronze Buddha statues dating mostly from the 18th century.

There are many images of the Buddha in *bhumisparsa mudra* – touching the earth to witness – and in the Calling for Rain *mudra,* standing on elongated pedestals in a highly stylised form, some octagonal, others hexagonal.

Inside the collection includes a rare Buddha image, seated in *dhyana mudra,* from Muang Sing in northern Laos, sinicised in style, with slanted eyes. Wearing an elaborate crown and robe it is lacquered and decorated with mother-of-pearl and semi-precious stones. Other religious artefacts inside include a magnificent manuscript chest, finely incised with foliate patterns, covered with lacquer and encrusted with glass mosaics of green, gold and garnet. The stylised floral decoration is is made up for flowers and medallions. The technique flourished in the north of Laos as well as in Lan Na and in Burma.

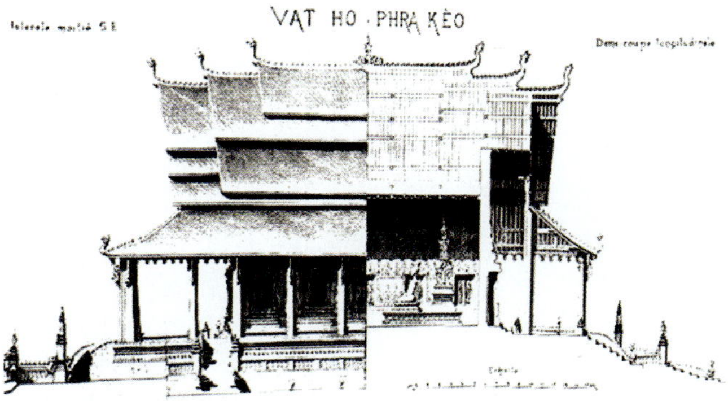

Drawing Wat Ho Phra Kaeo.

Left: *Wat Ho Phra Kaeo bronze Buddhas.*

Far left: *Wat Ho Phra Kaeo Buddha in* Bhumisparsa mudra.

Wat Si Muang

Location: Ban Simuang Setthathirath Road, leading to Friendship Bridge
Date: Originally 1563, rebuilt 1915 and 1956

This is a modern temple as the original, thought to have been constructed over an ancient Khmer Hindu shrine, was burned down during the Siamese raid of 1827. It was rebuilt in 1915 and again in 1956. Offerings are placed here as the temple is said to house the spirt of the city. The main *sim* contains the foundation pillar *lak muang* of Vientiane, a *lingam*-shaped pillar, brought by King Setthathirat (1548-71) in 1563 and regarded as the symbolic guardian of the city.

In the precincts of the *wat* an old laterite stupa was found by a scholar to have a carved stone relief that dates from the Khmer kingdom. Stylistically the relief is thought to resemble a carved image of Vajrapani at Phimai from the era of Jayavarman VI, (r. 1080-1107 AD), a period of Tantric Buddhism. Not contemporary with the stupa, it indicates the geographical extent of Khmer imperial rule to this part of Laos, although it may have been brought from Phimai and kept here with other sculptures. There is a statue of King Sisavangvong (reigned 1904-1959) in front of the *sim*.

Bronze Buddha in Bhumisparsa mudra*, Wat Si Muang.*

Wat Si Muang main entrance.

Location: Setthathirat Road
Date: 16th century, rebuilt 20th century

Wat Ong Teu

Built on an ancient site dating from the 3rd century, Wat Ong Teu was originally built by King Setthathirat during the 16th century. Its name, translated as the Temple of the Heavy Buddha, refers to a 16th century six metre tall bronze Buddha at the back of the *sim*, with smaller Buddha images on either side. The temple was destroyed by the Siamese invasion and rebuilt in the 20th century.

The Deputy Patriarch of the Monastic Order, Hawng Sangkhalat, resides here as Head of a Buddhist Institute visited by novice monks from all over Laos.

Wat Ong Teu, exterior.

Smaller Buddha images and offerings, Wat Ong Teu.

Location: Lane Xang Avenue
Date: 1964

Patuxai or Anousavari Monument (Victory Gate)

The grandiose Lao version of the Arc de Triomphe, known locally as the 'vertical runway' as it was made with cement donated by the Americans for the first airport runway, dominates the end of Lane Xang Avenue. Constructed between 1953-1964, it was originally called the Anousavari Monument and designed by Tham Sayasthsena, a Lao architect. It was known as the *Monument aux Morts* by the French. The monument has five towers which represent the five principles of coexistence among nations of the world. It is decorated with Lao mythological figures and demons from the *Phra Lak Phra Lam*, as well as images of the gods Vishnu, Brahma and Shiva in the centre. It commemorate lives lost during the struggle for independence from France and the Lao civil war between 1953-1975.

Any doubts about its aesthetic qualities are reinforced by a sign in English that proclaims: 'From a closer distance it appears even

Patuxai Monument. (RB)

less impressive, like a monster of concrete.' The lightbulbs held by concrete *apsaras* are at least energy efficient ones.

In 1975, the communist Pathet Lao changed the name to Patuxai, meaning gateway, in honour of their own victory. A pleasant park with water fountains have been created around it making it a focus for both local and foreign visitors.

Above: *Pratu Chai ceiling.* (RB)

Above left: *Detail of Pratu Chai ceiling.* (RB)

Location: Ban Mixay
Date: 1920s
Style: French colonial

Lao Textiles Gallery

This attractive colonial villa belonged to Madame Blanchard de la Brosse (1908-1984), *née* Souvannouvong, daughter of Prince Souvannouvong, a son of the last viceroy Boun Khong, and his Vietnamese wife, Nguyen Ti Ky Nam. She married the son of Monsieur Blanchard de la Brosse, the Governor of Cochinchina (after whom the The Museum of Vietnamese History in Saigon was originally named).

This handsome, two-storey house, framed in greenery, is set back from the road in a garden with palm trees and crimson bougainvillea. It is whitewashed and has a hipped roof with *cho faa* curling upwards in a temple style, with a pillared porch in the front left hand corner. There are long slender windows with blue louvred shutters. The interior has an inner and an outer wall, a construction that allowed cooling breezes to circulate around the building. As in many colonial buildings there are no hallways so the front door opens straight in to the ground floor showroom of the gallery, an elegant room with dark wood flooring and a wooden staircase, with long windows and shutters.

Lao Textiles Gallery.

Location: Thanon Lane Xane
Date: Late 20th century

Lao Presidential Palace

The building was first started in 1973 by the then Royal Lao government on the grounds that used to house the royal residence. It was designed by local architect Khamphoung Phonekeo but due to political change brought about by the takeover of the communist Pathet Lao in 1975, the building was not completed until much later. The Presidential Palace finally opened its doors in 1986 and even then only as a venue for government functions and ceremonies. The building is closed to the public.

It is a well-known landmark for its imposing beaux arts-style architecture complete with temple spires and shaded balconies. The building is surrounded by well-manicured lawns and gardens and fenced off by tall walls and a wrought iron gate.

The Presidential is not the official home of the Lao president which is located in the Vientiane suburb of Ban Phonthan. The palace is lit up in the evening and offers a great opportunity for night photography.

Vientiane Presidential Palace.

Lao National Museum

Location: Samsenthai Road
Date: 1925
Style: French colonial

Housed, somewhat ironically, in a colonial building that was once the residence of the French governor, this museum was called the Revolutionary Museum and charted the troubled history of Laos in the 20th century. It has recently been upgraded as well as renamed. The ground floor shows exhibits displaying the history of Laos, including artefacts from archaeological sites such as the Plain of Jars. On the second floor is a recreation of parts of the temple of Wat Phu in Champasak in the south, with stone lintels and images of the god Shiva and Ganesha. There are also recreations and dioramas of villages and homes of ethnic minorities who live in the mountainous areas of Laos, and wooden houses containing cooking utensils, hammocks and textiles. Several glass cases hold palm leaf manuscripts and Buddha statues. The top floor has several rooms of fascinating old black and white photographs illustrating the country's history of warfare in the 20th century. Although poorly labelled in English, these are compelling records, with condemning references to 'French and American imperialists'. There are photos of, for example, Hmong ethnic tribes employed by the CIA holding firearms and learning to shoot, as well as photos of Ho Chi Minh meeting with various Pathet Lao leaders in the hills of Sam Neua. Images of bombs dropped and damage caused during the nine year secret war are sobering.

The Lao National Museum, front entrance.

Lao Textile Museum

Location: Nong Tha Tai, Vientiane

In the Chantaboury neighborhood, on the outskirts of the city, is a collection of textiles in a private museum, The Lao Textile Museum. Composed of four traditional wooden Lao houses on stilts, of which only one is antique, the museum is in a verdant tropical garden setting with coconut palm trees, tamarind, papaya, jacaranda and fresh herbs, as well as fish ponds and a barn containing an old sugar cane press and large ceramic pots with dyeing facilities for indigo and displays of folk art.

The main house, which is more than a hundred years old, is hand carved teak with stilts and decorated with a steeply pitched roof. It has wooden floor frame looms beneath its stilts, in the traditional way, which can be taken apart and brought upstairs in the rainy season. It is a veritable treasure trove of Lao antiques, wooden artefacts, Buddha images, musical instruments, furniture such as chests and wardrobes and, above all, a fine collection of

Indigo Preparation, Textile Museum.

Textile Museum Vientiane.

hundreds of silk textiles gathered over decades by the owner and director, Hansana Sisane, son of Sisana Sisane, former Minister of Information and Culture, and his family.

In the aftermath of Laos' tragic history in the 1970s when the country was devastated by bombing (*see chapter History*), many family heirlooms including unique silk pieces were bought by foreign collectors and taken abroad to countries such as Australia and France. To preserve his country's vanishing artistic heritage, Sisane started collecting as many antique fabrics as possible, such as jackets, ceremonial skirts, *phaa sin,* sashes, *phaa biang*, hats, wall hangings, blankets, baby carriers, banners, pillowcases and sacred manuscript covers from the many ethnic minorities in the regions of Xieng Khouang, Attopeu, Houaphan as well as Luang Prabang. He collected tribal jewellery such as silver earrings, bracelets and necklaces such as torques, handed down through generations.

One section of the Museum includes the Lao-Japan Traditional Cultural Education Centre established for teaching languages, weaving, music, traditional customs and arts and crafts.

Right: *Costume, Lao Textile Museum.*

Vang Vieng

Vang Vieng is in Vientiane Province about 160 kilometres north of the capital. The town lies on the banks of the Nam Song (Nam Xong) river. The area is of outstanding natural beauty with dramatic limestone karst peaks rising sheer from the ground in the landscape surrounding the town. They abound in limestone caves, fed by a natural spring, with crystal clear waterfalls and pools. Originally named Mouang Song after the deceased King Phra Nha Phao of Phai Naam was seen floating down the river, the town was renamed Vang Vieng during French colonial rule in the 1890s.

Vang Vieng town. (RB)

A pedestrian bridge across the Nam Song river, Vang Vieng. (RB)

There are 16th and 17th century monasteries including Wat That and Wat Kang.

For a time the town became a haven for backpackers and young travellers, which some felt spoiled the atmosphere of this area of outstanding natural beauty. Of late the government has taken measures to ensure harmony has been restored. The town is well placed between Luang Prabang and Vientiane and those travelling by road sometimes stop here to admire the dramatic limestone cliffs and sweeping Nam Song river. There are five caves worth exploring near the town including Tham Chang and Tham Poukham. Hotels can arrange a tour. Do take a torch and admission fee is payable.

Luang Namtha

Devasted during the war years, Luang Namtha is a newly built town in an area inhabited by many ethnic minorities who live in the hills and mountains, wearing a great variety of hand woven cotton and silk garments, head-dresses and silver jewellery. They can be seen at the markets where they visit in the early mornings. Among them are the Hmong, who originate from the plains of Tibet and Mongolia, Lang Ten, Khamu, Tai Lu, Tai Dam and The Lang Ten minorities. Tai means 'people of', and is followed by

Luang Namtha town. (RB)

Main shopping street, Luang Namtha.

the area from which the people come. In these northern regions there are communities of Tai Daeng and Tai Dam, meaning red and black respectively. Their origins can be traced to the Red and Black Rivers in Yunnan in southern China. Other subgroups include the Tai Phuan, Tai Lue, Tai Moei, Tai Waat, Tai Nuea and Tai Khang.

Rice fields of Luang Namtha (© Khamla Chanthavong).

Muang Sing

This small town in northern Laos, 60 kilometres northwest of Luang Namtha, is in a picturesque location among mountains and streams. Once a small kingdom, it became part of French Laos in 1904 and still has a few colonial French buildings. At the morning market ethnic minorities, who come down to trade early, sell their weaving or produce grown in the mountains, wearing colourful hand woven clothes and elaborate head-dresses and silver. In particular, the Akha wear head-dresses covered in silver coins. Tai Lu and Tai Nua can also be seen here.

Muang Sing town. (RB)

Market day, Muang Sing. (RB)

A sale in progress. (RB)

Vendor carefully laying out her produce. (RB)

The Plain of Jars

A diminutive Madeleine Colani (third from right) with George Coedès and EFEO.

Close to the Laotian border with North Vietnam lie hundreds of gigantic, mysterious stone jars strewn across a deserted plateau called, simply, The Plain of Jars. Known in French as Plaine des Jarres, and in Laotian, Thông Haihin, this area in north-central Laos lies on the Xieng Khoang Plateau, part of the Annamite range of mountains. Flowing southward through the region is a tributary of the Mekong River, the Ngum River, and the landscape is characterised by narrow river valleys and steep sandstone and limestone hills ranging from 900 to 1,100 metres in elevation.

The ancient jars after which the area is named are rumoured to be more than 2,000 years old, and thought to be funerary urns. They are scattered right across the region, beyond the borders of Laos. During the French colonial regime, these were studied by pioneering French geologist, paleobotanist and archaeologist Madeleine Colani (1866-1943). This intrepid woman, born in Strasbourg, who earned her doctorate in Hanoi aged 54 years old, wrote her seminal work, *The Megaliths of Upper Laos*, in 1930. It is considered one of the great contributions to archaeological literature and is still used today by, among others, UNESCO. She and her equally intrepid sister Eleanor travelled all over French Indochina studying prehistoric sites. Colani's theory was that the megalithic stone jars were mortuary urns, used in funerary rites and practices of protohistoric communities in the area. Excavation at a cave at the Bang Ang jar field site, near Phonsavan, had revealed ash and bones and she concluded that it could have been a crematorium. The area could have been an ancient trading caravan route between eastern India, southern China and northern Vietnam. Nevertheless,

Ban Ang, Site 1, and Ban Soua, Site 2, on Plain of Jars were surveyed by Madeleine Colani in 1931, the only systematic documentation so far. She believed the jars related to ancient funerary practices.

Fragmentation and erosion of the jars is a problem. Most are on windswept mountain slopes with extremes of temperatures, being hot during the day and cold at night, and the exposure contributes to continuing damage of the jars. Farming and increased tourism are a threat to the sites.

Carved from sandstone, granite or limestone, the jars are thought to date from 5th century BC. Measuring up to three metres in height, they are predominantly barrel shaped. Some have flat rims.

the culture that created these vessels is shrouded in mystery. Research by Lao and Japanese archaeologists has only recently started up again but excavations by Dr Thongsa Sayavongkhamdi, Director-General of the Department of Museums and Archaeology at the Ministry of Information and Culture, reinforce Colani's theories.

The megalithic vessels, weighing up to 14 tons, with the tallest measuring three metres high, may be connected with the ancient Dong Son culture which originated close to Dien Bien Phu in Vietnam and flourished from 500 BC to 100 AD. Local legend tells of a military victory 1,500 years ago when an evil king, Chao Angka, so oppressed his people that they appealed to Khun Jeuam, a king in the north, to free them. He defeated Chao Angka and ordered the construction of the jars to make wine for the victorious celebration. The colourful tale, however, is unsubstantiated by any scholastic theory.

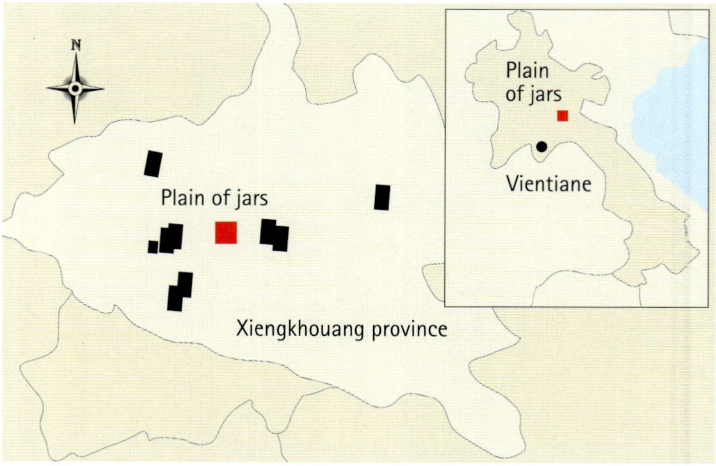

The Plain of Jars site and inset on map of Laos.

Most jars are made of sandstone, others of granite, conglomerate or calcified coral. While many jars are without decoration, some have incised representations of human faces or figures and monkeys and tigers. Many are round in shape while others angular, and a few have disks that appear to be lids. Circular stone discs found nearby are also thought to be lids. Tools and human remains found in the vicinity suggest manufacture and usage over many centuries. The jars may have been transported by elephants to different sites around an area of 50 kilometres. Archaeologists working for UNESCO have counted over 3,000 jars scattered across 90 sites in Xieng Khouang province. Visitors can view three sites. The first, Thong Hai Hin, has 298 jars of varying sizes, dominated by the huge King's Jar, the largest found so far. Site Two, known as Hai Hin Phu Salatao, has 68 jars and Site Three, called Hai Hin Laat Khai, has 80 jars.

But the other sites are off limits because of a more recent legacy: unexploded bombs. Between 1964 and 1973, a nine year 'secret war' led by the United States' Central Intelligence Agency was waged over Laos (*see Chapter 3*). The Plain of Jars (known as PDJ from its French name) became a war zone for the North Vietnamese fighting the Royal Lao government and was subjected to heavy bombing by the United States. About 1,100,000 tons of bombs fell on the Ho Chi Minh Trail and 500,000 tons on northern Laos, making Xieng Khouang Province one of the most heavily bombed places on earth. A third of these failed to explode. There are undetonated bombs, land mines and other unexploded ordnance in a quarter of the province's total land area that threaten the lives of local people. The British Mines Advisory Group (MAG), cleared 38.7 million square metres of suspect land between 2004 and 2012, destroying 161,802 items of UXO. As a result, 450,894 beneficiaries gained more safe land for farming, clean drinking water, latrines, irrigation for rice cropping, safe school compounds and tertiary roads. In 2012 the United States Congress expanded assistance in the UXO sector to $9.2 million dollars, almost doubling the previous year's funding.

Xieng Kouang is home to several ethnic minorities who practise agriculture here. Urns are sometimes used for farming debris. There are beliefs relating to the spirits that inhabit the jar fields.

Wat Si Phum Temple, Xieng Kouang.

House partly made of bomb casings (see foundations).

A macabre side effect of this legacy is the way villagers ingeniously recycle war scrap. Bomb casings are turned into fences, water troughs and even stilts for the palm-thatched wooden houses. The area has little agricultural or economic importance and the valleys and scrub covered hills are inhabited by Khmu and Hmong ethnic minorities who practise subsistence agriculture.

In 1998, UNESCO, the Lao Government and Xieng Khouang Province started a multi-year phased programme to safeguard and develop the Plain of Jars. They are seeking World Heritage nomination for the Plain of Jars archaeological landscape.

Tourism is now a major factor of the Lao economy and includes excursion to jar sites as well as local ethnic minority villages and historic areas associated with the Indochina wars. Visitors stay in Phonsavanh which replaced the flattened provincial capital, Xieng Khouang. Sadly, not a single example of Xieng Khouang temple architecture, one of the three original categories created by Henri Parmentier, who visited in 1923, remains intact. Only broken columns and a large Buddha loom at Wat Si Phum in old Xieng Khouang.

Wat Phu. (PP)

WAT PHU CHAMPASAK

To arrive at Wat Phu by boat on the Mekong river enhances the sense of discovery of a lost world, for part of the magic of this temple is its setting. The crumbling ruins of the Khmer temple, the foundations of which are pre-Angkorian and date back to the 6th century, lie in a majestic mountain setting on the banks of the Mekong where it widens gracefully before cascading into waterfalls, in southern Laos, eight kilometres southwest of Champasak and 37 kilometres downstream from the provincial capital of Paksé. Wat Phu means mountain temple and the religious monument was constructed in an area of dramatic natural beauty to mirror its sacred significance. It was nominated as a UNESCO World Heritage Site in 2001.

The site was discovered by French official Francis Garnier in 1866 when he explored the Mekong and French scholars studied the ruins. Excavations in 1995 revealed several levels of terraces beneath ground level. The area was the cradle of the pre-Angkorian kingdom of Chenla. Epigraphic evidence reveals that there was a capital, Bhavapura, in the vicinity, founded by King Bhavavarman I, originally a prince from Funan. He married into the royal family of Chenla and became its ruler. The sacred site was revered by all the Khmer kings who considered it to be the origin of the Khmer dynasties.

Wat Phu is an introduction to the glory of Khmer art. The ruined structures that remain date from the 10th-12th centuries. They are set against a backdrop of the Phu Kao mountain, sometimes called Phu Passak, 1,416 metres high, named 'Lingaparvata', meaning mountain of the *linga,* the phallic symbol of Shiva which held the divine essence, the energy of the universe. The Khmers, who absorbed Hinduism via merchants trading from India, worshipped Shiva, Vishnu and Brahma, and adopted the *linga* as the palladium of their kingdom. Archaeologists believe that some of these structures were built by Suryavarman II, who ruled Angkor between 1113 and 1150 and for whom Angkor Wat was constructed. Wat Phu was dedicated to Bhadreshvara, one of the names of Shiva.

Wat Phu seen across Mekong River. (PP)

Wat Phu was laid out in a linear form, as successive enclosures in a row, as opposed to Angkor, where enclosures surround each other concentrically. The Khmer temple was a replica of the Hindu cosmos in stone. The walls represented the edge of the world, the surrounding moat the cosmic ocean, and the central sanctuary the holy Mount Meru, abode of the gods.

There is a processional stone causeway, 250 metres long, once lined with lions, boundary stones and *nagas*, possibly built in the 11th century by Jayavarman VI, who created religious foundations at numerous sites within the Khmer empire. There are two large rectangular reservoirs, *baray*, the main 600 metres by 180 metres, filled with water, used for sacred and secular

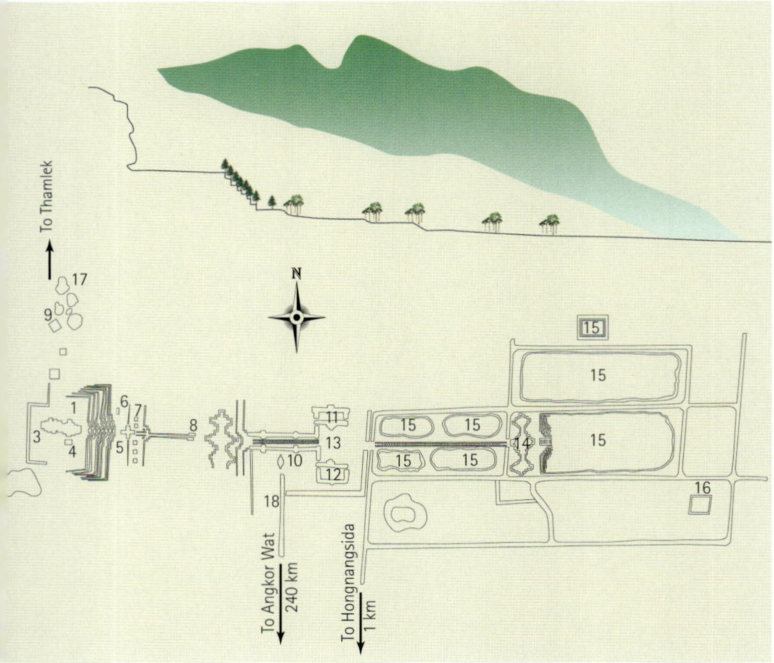

Wat Phu Monument

1. Sanectuary
2. Spring
3. Portico
4. Library
5. Susyaining wall
6. The God
7. Stupa
8. Dvarpala
9. Crocodile
10. Nandin Hall
11. Northern Hall
12. Southern Hall
13. Holly Road
14. Platform
15. Baray
16. Repository Exhibition Hall
17. Elephant
18. Ancient Road

Sandstone pavillion or 'palace'.

Sandstone pavillion or 'palace'.

Sanctuary with balustrade windows. (PP)

Southern 'palace' with stone processional causeway. (PP)

Pediment with Shiva and Uma on Nandi. (PP)

Devata flanking main entrance of sanctuary. (PP)

purposes. On either side, at the foot of the hill, are two impressive sandstone pavilions, or 'palaces', which may have been for segregated worship, probably 12th century.

The pavilions, currently under restoration, are sufficiently well preserved to reveal the architectural features of classical Khmer architecture. There are balustraded windows, porticos with triangular shaped pediments with two curving sides framing a tympanum, and carved lintels.

Beyond these lie the Nandi Pavilion, dedicated to the sacred bull Nandi, mount of Shiva, that has been restored, its laterite foundation platform dismantled and reassembled in 2011.

Up a stone pathway is the small central sanctuary, the main temple, with a restored library, parts of which probably date to the 10th century. Here there are remarkable *bas-reliefs* and carved lintels depicting the Churning of the Ocean of Milk, one of the most important Khmer myths, with Vishnu Sleeping on the Serpent Ananta. Others depict goddesses, *devatas*, and scenes from the *Ramayana*. A pediment shows a *bas-relief* thought to be of Bhima splitting Dhushasana. The temple houses an altar where the Shiva *linga* originally stood. The mountain behind has a rock deeply carved *Trimurti* showing the Hindu trinity with multi-armed Shiva in the centre flanked by a kneeling Vishnu and Brahma. Here there is a spring where the water, considered sacred, seeps out from overhanging rock and flows along a stone duct to sprinkle the sacred *linga* during ceremonies.

Wat Phu was a holy site not only for the Khmers but also for the Chams, the early Hinduised empire of central Vietnam. Today it is

Lintel southern door, Central Sanctuary, Indra on three-headed mount the elephant Airavata. (PP)

Indra with three headed Airavata. (PP)

still venerated and in February thousands of Lao pilgrims, both Hindu and Buddhist, congregate here for the annual full moon festival, a three day event.

As this is a living landscape, a Champasak Heritage and Cultural Landscape Protection Zone has been set up which includes cultivated agricultural lands and 55 villages.

Nearby are two other Khmer sites, Ho Nang Sida and Hong Tha Tao, dating from the 10th century. A kilometre south of Wat Phu, the sites are in ruins but are atmospheric.

Trimurti with Shiva with kneeling Vishnu and Brahma. (PP)

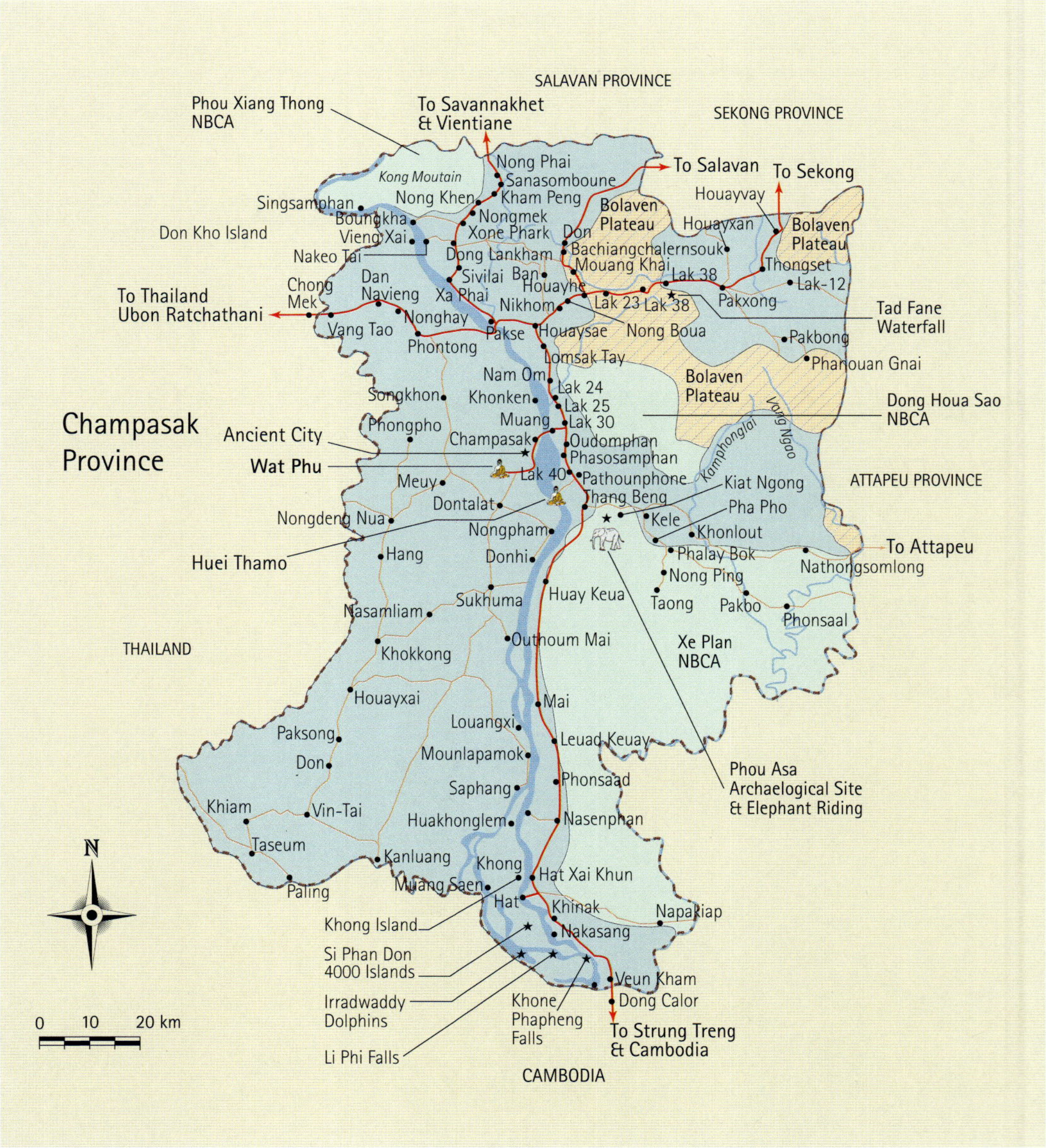

Paksé

Capital of the province of Champasak, Paksé was built by the French, starting in 1904. There are several notable colonial villas and Art Deco buildings. The Champasak Historical Heritage Museum is a French style building, with two storeys and eight gilded columns. It contains a collection of interesting sandstone artefacts on the ground floor such as Khmer lintels and statues, including 7th century lintels from Oum Muong. In particular there is a 7th century lintel resembling one discovered during excavation at Wat Phu. With *makaras* on either side spewing a decorative arch with a medallion in the centre, it is similar to styles found at the Khmer site of Sambor Prei Kuk, according to Claude Jacques in *The Khmer Empire*. There are textiles and jewellery from ethnic minorities in the region, musical instruments and pottery. The second floor contains photos of the revolutionary period and the Pathet Lao.

A french colonail building in Paksé. (RB)

Left: *Map of Champasak province, Wat Phu is marked (centre).*

Paksé Champasak Palace Hotel.

The vast Champasak Palace Hotel with its 115 rooms over six storeys was built as a palace by Prince Boun Oum of Champasak (1912-1980). He renounced his role as Head of the House of Champasak to become Prime Minister of Laos from 1948-50 and 1960-62 but then withdrew from politics. His palace is in a flamboyant French Art Deco style, covered in hand painted tiles with a Lao temple style roof with *cho faa.* The Prince spent very little time here as he fled into exile in France in 1974 before it was finished. After the revolution, construction was completed and it became a venue for Communist Party congresses and then in 1995 was converted into a hotel.

An aerial view of the Champasak Palace hotel, clearing showing the Lao temple style roof with Cho faa.

Opposite: *Rough Plan of Oum Moung.*

Huei Thamo – Oum Muong

Across the river, almost a kilometre wide at this point, on the eastern banks lie the ruins of another Khmer temple, Huei Thamo sometimes called Oum Muong, deep in the forest, accessible by a trail. Dating possibly from 10th-13th centuries, the remains, built of laterite, are completely covered in jungle, with laterite walls, carved columns half buried in the ground, and a large, moss covered seven-headed *naga* at the entrance. A small shrine on a hill contains a pillar over a metre high with carved heads, one a *Muchalinga*. Oum Muong is a veritable lost domain in the tropical forest.

Oum Moung.

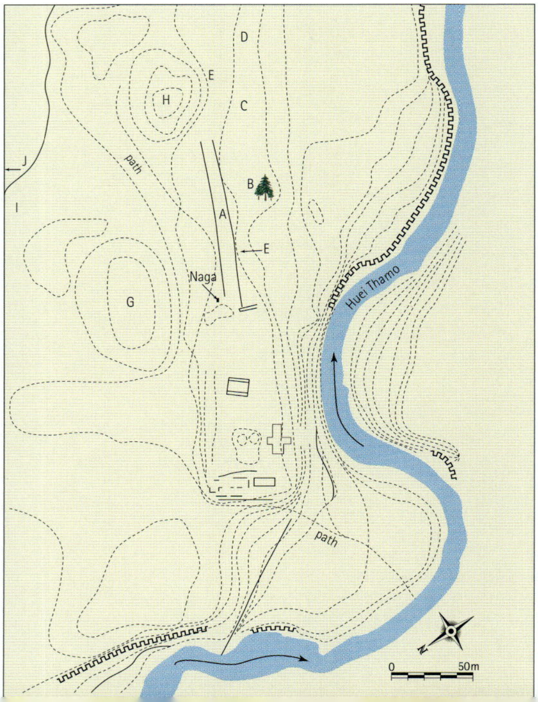

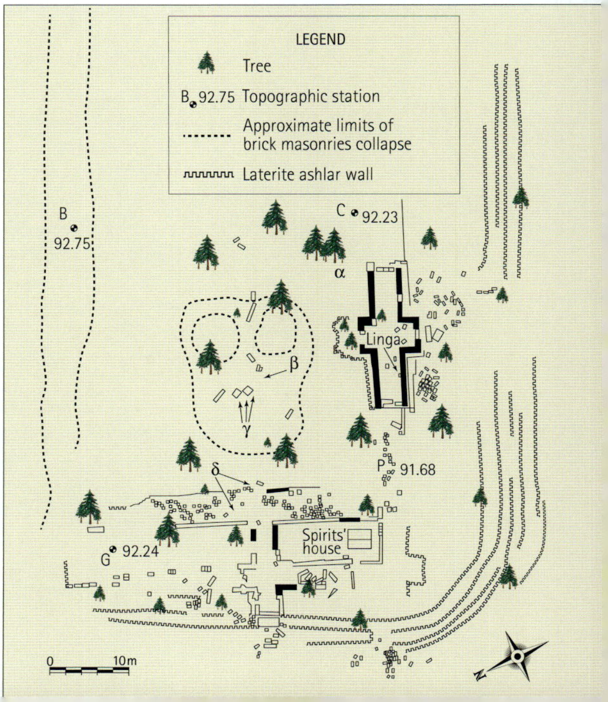

Living Arts

Living Arts

An old photo of two girls sewing.
(Courtesy University of Illinois)

"Intangible cultural heritage is ephemeral. It has no permanence and exists only for a set time and dies with the last note or the last line … as in poetry, or songs, handed down in the oral tradition."
UNESCO

Silk

"The sound of the waterfall, little sister mine, is like the humming of your spinning-wheel." Lao song

Textiles are more than an art form, they are a manifestation of cultural identity, and nowhere is this more so than in Laos. Silk weaving was a tradition handed down from mother to daughter through the centuries. According to legend, it was taught originally by the guardian spirits, through the intermediary of Khun Burôm, the god of the sky, said to have begat Fa Gnum. Silkweaving was a fundamental part of the way of life, linked to Buddhist rites and animist practices, and carried out in rhythm with the annual cycle of rice growing.

The silk industry in Laos has a long and illustrious past for, according to ancient Chinese documents, the first people to produce silk, the Ailoa of southern China, are thought to be ancesters of the Lao. From the 2nd century BC onwards, this luxurious commodity was transported from southern and central China across to India, Baghdad, Syria and trading centres throughout the Middle East along caravan routes that became known as the Silk Route.

Opposite: *Chao Wam Fam, a consort of Prince Satou, early 20th century.*

But in Laos these historic skills almost vanished during the 1960s-70s when the country was drawn into the Vietnam war. In the devastating aftermath, women sold their heirlooms to collectors in order to feed their families. With the loss of these pieces, original patterns started to disappear. As older women ceased working, their inherited knowledge was lost to successive generations.

Little princesses. Note their beautiful skirts and jewellery.
(Courtesy Archives des Colonies Editions de Lodi)

Then, in the late 1980s, the Lao Women's Union was formed to try to preserve the weaving heritage and to generate income for rural women. They opened a gallery, The Art of Silk, in Vientiane, that was the sole public collection in the country. Today, that rich weaving tradition is once more an important part of Lao life, with the help of the Union, the United Nations, small enterprises and individuals.

One of them is American weaver Carol Cassidy and her gallery Lao Textiles. In 1989, she arrived as a 'Weaving Expert' for the United Nations Development Programme to provide technical assistance to Lao Cotton, a state run textile enterprise. She found a 'weaver's paradise' and set about working with silk weaving. As the communist government of Laos was starting to

Top left: *Hmong woman.*
Left: *A young hilltribe woman with a baby on her back.*
Top right: *A child in woven skirt.*
Above: *An Akha hill tribe woman.*

The weavers use techniques such as continuous and discontinuous supplementary warp and weft, interlock tapestry and warp (using cotton) and weft (using silk) ikat.

Weft ikat, or *mat mi,* is the technique of resist-dyeing the weft (the thread carried by the shuttle), by tying groups of wefts with natural or plastic bindings. This is practised throughout Southeast Asia and comes from the Indonesian word *mengikat,* to tie or bind. The method is to wrap strands of raw silk on to a simple shaft frameloom, and then tie the strands with banana leaf threads or plastic bindings into patterns according to a plan in the weaver's mind. She selects two to six pairs of threads, comprising four to 12 individual threads. They are then slipped off the loom and placed in dye. The tied weft resists dye penetration when immersed. When the bindings are removed, the undyed parts form a pattern. Wax is sometimes smeared on top to assist the resist process. The silk is remounted on the frame to be re-tied for the other colours in the pattern, as many as five or six times, corresponding to the number of colours in the design. The main colour is dyed first, followed by secondary colours. Base colour silk is strung lengthwise on to the loom, usually a frame loom, with tongue and groove, which can be dismantled and stored if necessary. The silk is then woven into an array of motifs of flowers, animals, birds, fruits, temples, mythological images, Hindu and Buddhist symbols, ships, stars and geometric designs, some so ancient that they are attributed to the Vietnamese Dong Son culture of 500 BC.

Rural farms raise silk as an agricultural product. The cycle of silk production harmonises with that of rice growing, so that when land is prepared for the rice crop in the dry season, mulberry trees are pruned. When the monsoon rains begin, rice seedlings are planted and cotton is sown, while silkworms are raised from the silk moths' eggs. Mulberry trees proliferate in mountainous regions such as Luang Prabang, and it is on the leaves of this tree, of two species, the *Morus alba* and *Morus australis,* that silkworms feed. The best silk is made by the caterpillar of the *Bombyx mori* silk moth, which exist only in captivity, on sericulture farms. The *Bombyx mori* silk moth lays its eggs in the dry season, from October to May. In spring they are moved to a warm area where they hatch after two or three weeks.

Weavers at work.

A woman weaving underneath her house.

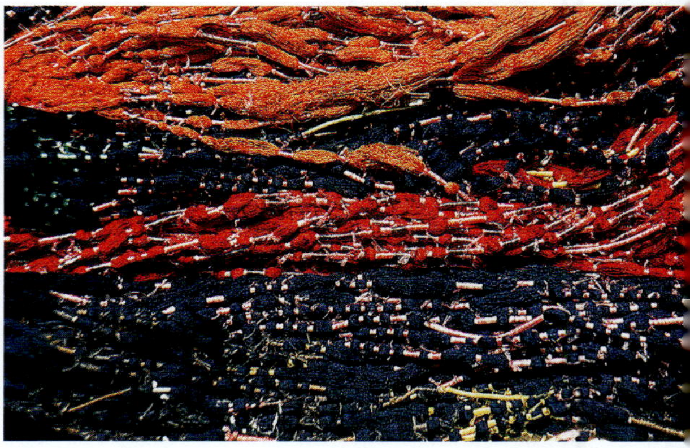

Various stages in the production of silk thread.
From top to bottom left: *silkworms, the cocoons, boiling the cocoons;* from top to bottom right: *spinning into thread, tie-dye and silk skeins.*

Opposite: *Some of the diverse patterns in Lao silk.*

This woman at a spinning wheel probably also weaves her family's clothes.

Right: *A girl wearing traditional Laos silk, scarf,* phaa biaeng.

Laos silk patterns.

Each egg hatches into a caterpillar which feeds on the mulberry leaves and grows. Young silkworms consume up to 30,000 times their own weight. After about 26 days they are plump and white and ready to spin a silk cocoon. This is made when the silkworm squirts liquid out of its spinneret, a hole in its lower lip, which forms a single fine filament about 300-500 metres long. The length of a strand of silk produced by a cocoon weighing around 3 grams can vary from 300 to more than a thousand metres. Inside, its body changes into a pupa.

The cocoons are then collected and placed in hot water that kills the worm, or pupa, and loosens the filaments. The process of killing the worms is not practised by strict Theravada Buddhists. Instead, if the pupa is not killed but left to die naturally, the silk is pulled out of the cocoon, by combing it out, and is not one single long filament. This is known as wild or raw silk. If the insects were left to develop, they would change into moths, bite their way out of the cocoons and break the long silk thread. Some adult moths are allowed to develop in order to lay the next batch of eggs. These raw fibres are covered with seracin, a waxy substance, that feels coarse. Boiling in water and soda ash, and then drying in the sun, removes most of it so that the fibres can be spun. The high seracin content of Lao silk produces threads that are uneven, giving them a beautiful, varied texture.

About a dozen filaments are reeled together to form a single thread. The thread is then wound on to reels. Silk workers gather the strands from several cocoons and fix them to a reeling

machine. The machine unravels the cocoons, twists the strands together and winds the yarn on to a reel. At this stage the silk yarn is known as raw silk. It is taken off the reels and twisted into bundles called skeins. Then the skeins of silk are ready to be dyed.

Silk production is laborious and fraught with dangers as worms may succomb to insects, mosquitos or disease, so they must be maintained in a hygienic environment and closely monitored. It takes between 2,500 to 3,000 cocoons to make one metre of fabric and the process is very labour intensive. Weight for weight, silk is stronger than steel and has countless applications.

Vegetable dyes were used, including yellow from the turmeric root, *Curcuma domestica,* and from jackfruit trees, *Artocarpus rigidus,* and also from the leaves of eucalyptus, *Eucalyptus citriodora;* pink from tree bark; brown from coconut husk; carmine red from cochineal beatles; crimson from the secretion, *lac,* of an insect *kerria lacca;* black from seed pods of the ebony tree, *Diaspyros mollis;* green from indigo leaves, *Indigofera tinctoria;* and blue from the indigo plant, when the leaves are soaked with limestone. The plants are boiled to release the colours and the silk, a pale bleached colour in its natural state, absorbs these natural dyes. Indigo bleeds and fades with age, although the faded look is now in fashion. Today, artificial dyes are also used.

The renewed interest in weaving has helped the tourism industry, prompting many more pieces being to be made for sale at venues such as the new Hmong market held every

Hill tribe women sell their embroidery at the Hmong market (below) *which is held after sunset on Sisavangvong Road.*

Silversmiths at work.

evening in the main street of Luang Prabang. At galleries such as OckPopTok in Luang Prabang demonstrations of silkweaving take place and high quality pieces are available for sale.

All of these factors represent the revival of a precious national heritage. The creation and development of weaving techniques are vital to perpetuating the expertise of weavers and contribute to the evolution of Lao culture.

Silver

Silversmithing is another traditional skill that is being revived in Luang Prabang. As well as being a form of physical embellishment and adornment, jewellery had a vital historical significance. It was a store of portable wealth. It also had talismanic qualities, as silver set with certain stones was endowed with magical powers and would protect the wearer. Silversmiths were traditionally priests of some rank. Laotian silversmiths specialise in ornate filigree work, but they often lack the chemicals needed to polish their work to a high sheen. The silver comes from within Laos and from China. It varies in purity from 50% to 100%, with many decorative items being 90%. Soft pure silver is hardened by alloying, usually with copper, as in the case with sterling silver, which has a minimum silver content of 92.5%.

In *The Yao,* Jess Pourret examines the cultural significance of silver among this group. It keeps the soul within the body, they believe, and plays an important role in social and economic life, especially at marriage. Silver is paid by the groom or his family to a bride's family. Many hill tribes in the Luang Prabang area wear highly ornate silver jewellery that enhances their elaborate costumes. These consist of earrings, necklaces, bracelets, rings, silver coil hems on tunics, silver breast plaques, and turbans decorated with bands of silver coils and chains. Tools used in

silver working include the hammer, punch, chisel, cutters, cleaning, polishing and soldering agents and a small forge with hand activated bellows. Techniques include casting, hammering, chiselling and repoussé work in low relief, champlevé, chasing and etching. Until a few decades ago enamel was used in cloissoné and champlevé work for objects such as earrings, pendants, rings and bracelets. They would melt down silver ingots, or old silver, including coins, some dating from the French era.

Royal dancer. (RB)

Dance and Music

"Those who eat sticky rice, live in dwellings mounted on piles, and play the khene, these without any doubt are Laotians" Lao proverb

Music, dance and theatre are influenced by the Siamese and Khmer traditions. The royal court at Luang Prabang probably adopted the Khmer classical court culture, although on a more modest scale. This would have included dance and the *Ramayana* epic, the *Phra Lak Phra Lam.* An important part would be the masked dance, *khon,* and shadow theatre, with an orchestra, *piphat*, of percussion instruments of gong carillons on a circular frame, *khong wong,* bamboo xylophones, *ranat,* cymbals, *sing,* reed oboe, *pi,* and drums, *khlong.* All musical instruments, especially drums, possess a *khuan,* a soul. Hence a special drum shrine is part of most temple compounds.

A musician playing the ranat *or bamboo xylophone.*

In his work *Temple Drums,* Charles Archaimbault, a member of the École Française d'Éxtrême-Orient from 1951-1978 who studied ethnology and festivals in Laos, wrote that "music is considered as one of the arts belonging to *p'isanuk'uka',* in other

Opposite below: *Dancers in their full costume.* (Courtesy Archives des Colonies Editions de Lodi)

Below: Phra Lak Phra Lam *performance.* (Courtesy University of Illinois)

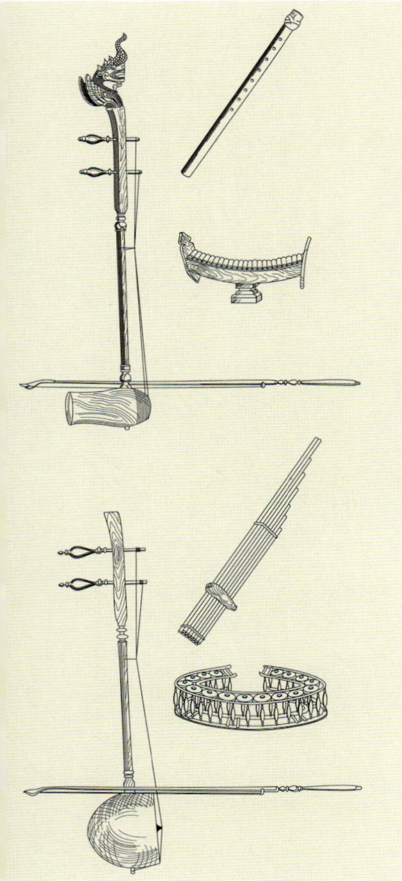

Lao musical instruments.
Left top and bottom: So I *and* So O.
Right from top to bottom: Khouy, ranat, khene *and* Khong wong.

Phra Lak, Hanuman and Phra Lam. (Courtesy University of Illinois)

words to the god of Techniques." He referred to the soul of the instruments and to the importance of the royal orchestras who placed their instruments in special pavilions to prevent the *khuan* from escaping.

The *khene,* a bamboo instrument with a double row of bamboo reeds in a hardwood sound box, was introduced into the *piphat* orchestra much later, infusing the music with a uniquely Lao sound and mood. It is one of the characteristic elements of Lao culture and nowadays folk music is centred on the *khene.* There are three different varieties of *khene:* the six hole, the 14 hole and the 16 hole instrument. Decorated *khene* are called *khene lay,* and plain ones are *khen puak.* These are blessed and the spirit of the *khene* is appeased with flowers and candles. Music is not written down but is learned aurally and handed down. Folk music is usually accompanied by dance and theatre, sometimes rather raucous and bawdy.

Lam is the characteristic folk song of Laos, with numerous regional variations. It draws on ancient stories and is imbued with notions of spirit communication.

Prince Souvannaphouma (1901-1984), former Prime Minister of Laos, wrote about Lao music and its role in daily life: "Fond of gaiety, the Laotian has a true passion for music, and in Laos, songs and concerts form part of every festival."

Lam vong.

The People's Democratic Republic has allowed a local dance company in Luang Prabang to call itself The Royal Ballet again, and they perform in the former Assembly Building within the palace grounds. This has proved popular with visitors to the ancient royal capital.

The dance resembles Khmer and Siamese dance dramas, composed of solo numbers or small groups of performers, who were

Above and below: *Dancers from the Royal Ballet Theatre.* (Courtesy University of Illinois)

traditionally female, dressed either in glittering dance costumes of spun gold or in regional costumes. Old black and white photographs of the king's dance troupes show them attired in extravagant brocade outfits, gold coronets and abundant jewellery.

Art projects and festivals have been organised, such as The Continuum Asia Project, part of TheatreWorks Ltd, led by artistic director Ong Keng Sen from Singapore. They have brought together surviving elders from the Lao *Ramayana* dance tradition with the young people of Luang Prabang to stage revivals of the Lao version of this great Hindu epic. In one historic revival in 2003, the Royal Ballet Theatre and an independent organisation of young people, assisted by TheatreWorks, performed three episodes of the nine episode *Phra Lak Phra Lam.* Until the 1960s, the *Phra Lak Phra Lam* used to be performed by the young people of Luang Prabang in front of the palace for the king. Now The Royal Ballet perform most evenings in the former Assembly Building within the palace grounds (see illustration p. 169).

There is also folk dance throughout Laos, *fon phum muong,* with a varied repertoire, and the popular *lam vong,* the traditional dance with its slow rhythm and stylised hand movements, performed by everyone at festivals. Dances celebrate a range of events from bountiful harvest to courtships and weddings. Folk theatre, *mohlam luong,* is another tradition, and folk opera, *likay,* and puppetry, *lakhon tukkata,* similar to other countries in the Southeast Asian region. In particular, the *lakhon tukkata* belonged to the ceremonial traditions of the royal court, with rod-puppets, *ipok,* that were kept in Wat Xieng Thong. These performances were imbued with religious significance and customs, and every show was preceded by prayers to the ancestors and *gurus.*

Hotels and Restaurants in Laos

LUANG PRABANG

Hotels

Below is a selection of recommended 5 star and 4 star hotels. New ones appear regularly, so the list is not exhaustive. There are also many small boutique hotels and guesthouses in every price range.

Amantaka $$$$$
P.O. Box 1090, Luang Prabang, Lao P.D.R
Tel: +856 71 860333 / Fax: +856 71 860335
Tel: 071 860 333
www.amanresorts.com

The Luang Say Residence $$$$$
4-5 Ban Phonepheng, P.O. Box 507
Luang Prabang, Lao PDR
Tel: +856 (0) 71 260 891
www.luangsayresidence.com

La Résidence Phou Vao $$$$$
3 PO Box 50
Luang Prabang PDR 84330
Tel: + 856 71 212194
www.residencephouvao.com

Hotel de la Paix $$$$$
Manomai Street,
Ban Mano, Luang Prabang, 0600
Tel: +856 71 260 777 Fax: +856 71 260 776
Email: book@hoteldelapaixlp.com
www.hoteldelapaixlp.com

Grand Luang Prabang $$$$
Ban Xiengkeo Luang Prabang 1191
Tel: +856 712538517
www.grandluangprabang.com

Alila Luang Prabang $$$$$
Unit 4, Ban Mano Old Prison Road
Tel: + 856 71 260 777
Email: luangprabang@alilahotels.com
www.alilahotels.com

Satri House $$$$$
057 Photisarath Rd, Ban That luang,
Tel: (071) 253-491 Fax: +856 71 253 418
www.satrihouse.com

Trois Nagas $$$$
Ban Vatnong, Sakkarine Road
Tel: +856 71 253 888
Email: book@3-nagas.com
www.3-nagas.com

Xieng Thong Palace $$$$
Tel: + 856 71 213 200
www.xiengthongpalace.com

Villa Maly $$$$
Tel: +856 (0) 71 253 903-904
www.villa-maly.com

Villa Santi $$$$
Tel: (071) 252 157
www.villasantihotel.com

Maison Souvannaphoum $$$$
Tel: (071) 212-577
www.angsana.com

Apsara Rive Droite $$$
Tel (071) 254-670
www.theapsara.com

Auberge Calao $$$
P.O.Box: 7158.
Tel: +856 21 218972-4. Fax. +856 21 216387. E-
www.calaoinn.laopdr.com/

Mekong Riverview Hotel $$$
Mekong Riverside Road, Xieng Thong Village
P.O. Box 183, Luang Prabang,
Tel: +856 (0) 71 25 49 00
Fax: +856 (0)71 25 48 90
www.mekongriverview.com

Saynamkhan River View $$$
Kingkitsalath Road, Ban Wat Sene
Tel: +856 71212976
Fax: +856 71253719
Email: saynamkhanhotel@gmail.com
www.saynamkhanhotel-luangprabang.com

Palais Juliana $$$$
Chao Phetsalath Street,
Ban-Sangkalok
Luang Prabang
www.lepalaisjuliana.com
Tel: +856 71 260417
Fax: +856 71 254542
info@lepalaisjuliana.com

Restaurants

L'Elephant
contact@elephant-restau.com
Tel: + 856 71 252 482
Fax: + 856 71 252 492

Tamarind
Ban Vat Sene
info@tamarindlaos.com
Tel: 971 213 128

Coconut Garden
Sisavong Road
coconutgarden@elephant-restau.com
Tel: + 856 71 252 482
Fax: + 856 71 252 492856 71 252 482

Apsara
Tel: + 856 71 254 670
Email: info@theapsara.com
www.theapsara.com

Blue Lagoon
Ban Choumkhong
Tel: +856 71 253 698
www.blue-lagoon-café.com

Mekong Riverview
Xieng Thong Village
Tel: + 856 (0) 71 25 49 00
www.mekongriverview.com/en/contact.html

Tamnak Lao
Ban Vat Sene
Tel: +856 71 252525, (+856) 71 212239
www.tamnaklao.net

Villa Santi
Ban Vat Sene
+856 71 252 157
www.villasantihotel.com

VIENTIANE

Hotels

Settha Palace $$$$$
Tel: (021) 217 581
www.setthapalace.com

Green Park Hotel $$$$
248 Khouvieng Road,
Ban Nongchanch
Tel: +856 21 264 097
www.greenparkvientiane.com

Lao Plaza $$$$$
63 Samsenethai Road,
PO Box 6703
Tel: +856-21 218808
Fax: +(856 21) 218808 - 9
Email: lph@laoplazahotel.com
www.laoplazahotel.com

Ansara Hotel $$$$
Quai Fa Gnum, Ban Vat Chan Tha, Hom 5
Muang Chanthabury Vientiane
Tel: +856 21 213 514
www.ansarahotel.com

Don Chan Palace $$$$
Sistanak District
Tel: 021/244-288
www.donchanpalacelaopdr.com

Vayakorn Inn Vientiane $$
019, Hengbounnoy Street, Ban Haysoke,
Chanthabouly District, Vientiane
Tel: +856 21 215348, 215349
Fax: +856 21 215347
Email: info@vayakorn.biz; vayakorn@gmail.com
www.vayakorn.biz

Restaurants

Kop Chai Deux
54 Than Setthathirat
Tel: 21 251564

L'Opera
Nam Phu Fountain
Tel: 21 215099

Scandinavian Bakery
Nam Phu Fountain
Tel: 21 215199

Makphet
Thanon Setthathirat
Tel: 21 260587

Koua Lao
141 Samsenthai Road
Tel: 856 21 215 777

CHAMPASAK

Hotels

Champasak Palace Hotel $$$$
No.13th Rd, Ban Prabath, Pakse
Champasak Provine, P.O Box 718
www.champasakpalacehotel-pakse.com

La Folie Lodge $$$$
Done Daeng, District Pathoumphone, BP 668
Tel: +856 30 534 7603
www.lafolie-laos.com

BIBLIOGRAPHY

Bassenne, M., *In Laos and Siam*, Bangkok: White Lotus, 1912

Bickersteth, J. & Eliot, J., *Laos*, Bath: Footprints Handbook, 2002

Cassidy, C., *Beyond Tradition: Lao Textiles Revisited: The handwoven textiles of Carol Cassidy*, New York: Museum at the Fashion Institute of Technology, 1995

Chazee, L., *The Peoples of Laos, Rural and Ethnic Diversities*, Bangkok: White Lotus, 1995

Conway, S., *Silken Threads Lacquer Thrones – Lan Na Court Textiles*, Bangkok: River Books, 2002

Cooper, N., *France in Indochina: Colonial Encounters*, New York and Oxford: Berg, 2001

Cumming, J., *Laos*, Hong Kong: Lonely Planet Publications Pty Ltd, 1994

Cupet, P., *Travels in Laos and Among the Tribes of Southeast Indochina: The Pavie Mission Indochina Papers (1879-1895) Vol. 6*, Bangkok: White Lotus, 2000

De Berval, René, *Kingdom of Laos*, Saigon: France-Asie, 1959

De Carné, L., *Travels on the Mekong, Cambodia, Laos and Yunnan*, Bangkok: White Lotus, 1995

De Lagreé, D., *Voyage d'exploration*, 1866

Delaporte, L. & Garnier, F., *A Pictorial Journey on the Old Mekong: Cambodia, Laos and Yunnan: The Mekong Exploration Commission Report (1866-1868) Vol. 3*, Bangkok: White Lotus, 1998

Engelmann, F., *Luang Prabang: Capitale de Legendes*, Paris: ASA Editions, 1997

Evans, G., *A Short History of Laos*, Melbourne: Allen & Unwin, 2003

Fisher, R. E., *Buddhist Art and Architecture*, London: Thames & Hudson, 1993

Garnier, F., *Travels in Cambodia and Parts of Laos Vol. 1: The Mekong Exploration Commission Report (1866-1868)*, Bangkok: White Lotus, 1996

Giteau, M., *L'Art du Laos*, École Française d'Éxtrême-Orient, Livre Picard, 2001

Gosling, B., *Old Luang Prabang*, Oxford: Oxford University Press, 1997

Goudineau, Y. (ed.), *Laos and Ethnic Minority Cultures: Promoting Heritage*, Paris: UNESCO Publications, 2003

Griffiths, C., *Laos and Cambodia*, London: Insight Guides, 2000

Hall, T. & Mansfields, S., *Laos Hilltribes*, Oxford: Oxford University Press, 2000

Kremmer, C., *Bamboo Palace: Discovering the Lost Dynasty of Laos*, London: Harper Collins Publishers, 2003

Kremmer, C., *Stalking the Elephant Kings*, Hawaii: University of Hawaii Press, 1998

Lewis, N., *A Dragon Apparen: Travels in Cambodia, Laos and Vietnam*, London: Eland Books, 1982

Lopetcharat, S., *The Lao Buddha: The Image and Its History*, Bangkok: Siam International Book Company, 2000

Marchal, H., 'L'Art Decoratif au Laos', *Arts Asiatiques*, Vol. 10, No. 2, École Française d'Éxtrême-Orient: Paris, 1964

Mouhot, H., *Travels in the Central Parts of Indo-China (Siam), Cambodia and Laos, during the years 1858, 1859, and 1860*, Vols I, II, London: John Murray, 1864 (reprinted: Bangkok: White Lotus 1986)

Murphy, D., *One Foot in Laos*, London: John Murray, 1999

Parmentier, H., *L'Art du Laos*, Publications École Française d'Éxtrême-Orient: Paris, 1988

Pourret, J. G., *The Yao: The Mien and Mun Yao in China, Vietnam, Laos and Thailand*, Bangkok: River Books, 2002

Rawson, P., *The Art of Southeast Asia*, London: Thames & Hudson, 1967

Said, E., *Orientalism: Western Conceptions of the Orient*, London: Penguin Books, 1995

Stuart-Fox, M., *A History of Laos*, Cambridge: Cambridge University Press, 1997

www.efeo.fr/archives/archives.shtml

www.seasite.niu.edu/lao/culture/Luangprabang 2/treasures_of_luang_prabang.htm

FURTHER READING

Boonprasert, Sarun, *Khumue Nam Thiao Luang Prabang (Guidebook to Luang Prabang)*, Bangkok: Sarakadee, 2005

Boonyasurat, Worarak, *Cheun Chom Sathapat: Wat Nai Luang Phrabang (Architectural Appreciation of Temples in Luang Prabang)*, Bangkok: Muang Boran, 2003

Luang Prabang: An Architectural Journey, Vientiane: Ateliers de la Peninsule Co, Ltd. 2004

John Keay, *Mad About the Mekong*, Harper Collins, 2005

GLOSSARY

"When one has heard, one must listen, and when one has seen one must judge with one's heart"
Lao saying

Abhaya Buddha's pose symbolising the giving of reassurance

Abhidarma Philosophical discussions

Ananta Mythical serpent

Angkor Temple complex, former capital of the Khmer Empire in Cambodia, derived from the Sanskrit *nagara*, meaning holy city

Angkor Wat Most important temple at the site of Angkor

Asoka Buddhist king of India in 3rd century BC

Avatar Sanskrit for incarnation of a deity

Bang fai Rocket fireworks

Bangkok Capital of Siam, present day Thailand

Betelnut Nut of the areca palm tree used for chewing, mixed with lime paste and leaf of the betel-pepper plant

Bas-relief Two dimensional carving

Bhumisparsa Buddha's pose touching the earth

Bodhi tree Tree under which the Buddha received enlightenment

Bodhisattva Sanskrit for enlightened one who forgoes full enlightenment to help others

Brahmin Member of the Indian Hindu priestly caste

Buddha Meaning Enlightened One, founder of Buddhism, Prince Siddharta Gautama who lived in 6th century BC

Buddhism Religious beliefs based on the teachings of the Buddha

Cakravala Configuration of the world with Mount Meru at the centre

Champa The empire of the Cham people who occupied southern Vietnam

Champasak Kingdom of southern Laos

Chao faa Literally sky cluster, ornate finials on temples

Chiang Mai Kingdom of Northern Thailand

Cornice Upper part of an entablature

Corinthian Column of the classical order having bell shaped capital with rows of acanthus leaves

Dana The act of giving, virtue of Buddhism

Deva Buddhist deity, masculine

Devi Female deity

Devata Goddess Hindu and Buddhist *Devata luang* Major tutelary deity of a city state

Dharma Wheel Symbol of the preaching of the Buddha's first sermon

Dharmachakra Buddhist, Turning the wheel of the law

Dhyana The attitude of meditation

Dok so fa Decorative symbol of the universe placed on the roof of a temple

Erawan 33 headed elephant mount of Indra, the symbol of Laos, now depicted with three heads

Façade The front of a building

Ficus religiosa Tree under which the Buddha received enlightenment, the Bodhi tree

Finial Ornamental feature, of wood, at the top of a gable

Gable Triangular area of wall beneath the roof at the end of a building with a pitched roof

Garuda The mythical half bird, half man, which carried Vishnu on his back

Guru Spiritual Guide

Hanglin Bamboo instrument for the pouring of holy water over sacred images

Hanuman Monkey general in the Ramayana

Hau tai Stupa

Hinduism Polytheistic religion of India, one of the oldest in the world, and of the Khmer empire

Hmong Hilltribe of northern Laos

Hor kong Drum chapel in temple compound

Indochina French name for the Union of Laos, Cambodia and Vietnam

Indra Hindu god of war

Khmer People of Cambodia and of the Khmer Empire

Kinaree Mythical half human and half bird

Krishna An incarnation of the god Vishnu

Jataka Stories of the Buddha's lives

Karma Cause and effect of moral acts accumulated in this and future lives

Kutis Sacred library

Lan Na Kingdom of Northern Thailand, knnown as the Land of a Million Ricefields

Lane Xang 14th century kingdom, Land of a Million Elephants

Lao The Tai speaking people who settled in Laos

Laotian The people of Laos

Lao People's Democratic Republic Current name of communist Laos

Lintel A horizontal length of wood or stone carrying the weight of the wall above a door or window

Mahabharata Ancient Hindu epic from India

Mahayana Buddhism Branch of Buddhism adopted by northern Asia and by the Khmer Empire

Makaras Aquatic demons consuming themselves

Muang A city-state or principality

Muang Sawa Original name of Luang Prabang

Mudra Sacred gesture or pose of the Buddha

Mount Meru Home of the gods, a mountain at the centre of the universe

Moulding Ornamental carving on a wall's projections

Naga A multi-headed snake, a guardian deity

Nagarajas Snake kings

Newel The central post of a handrail on a staircase

Nirvana Literally nothingness, release from earthly ties

Nimbus a halo

Na No One of the tutelary spirits of Luang Prabang

Pali Ancient Indic language in which the Buddhist canon is written

Paramitas Virtues

Pathet Lao Lao Communist Party which took control of Laos in 1975

Pediment Triangular space formed by the ends of pitched roofs

Phi Spirit

Phi khoun wat Benevolent spirit of the wat.

Phra Lak Phra Lam Lao version of the Ramayana

Phra rabieng The monk's living quarters

Phu Si Sacred Mount in the middle of Luang Prabang

Pilaster A flat rectangular decorative column projecting slightly from a wall

Pitched Roof A sloping roof

Pra Bang The sacred Buddha image, of solid gold, palladium of Luang Prabang

Pu No Tutelary spirit of Luang Prabang

Raja King

Rama An incarnation of Vishnu, hero of the Indian epic, the Ramayana

Ramayana Ancient Hindu epic from India, adapted in Laos and called the Phra Lak Phra Lam

Samsara Unavoidable cycle of death and rebirth

Shiva The Hindu god of creation and destruction

Sita Wife of Rama in the Ramayana

Siamese Formerly the people from Siam, now Thailand

Sim The main congregation hall in a temple compound

Sinhalese Sri Lankan

Sip Song Pan Na Southern China, now Yunnan, once a kingdom, now called Xishuangbanna

Sri Lanka Former Ceylon

Stucco Plaster used on the face of a building to represent stonework

Stupa Buddhist reliquary monument, *stup* in Sanskrit means to gather together

Sukhothai Thai kingdom

Sutras Sermons of the Buddha (*sutra* literally means string or thread)

Tai Linguistic group of Laos and Thailand

That Structure for relics and ashes

Tripitaka Texts of the Buddhist canon

Theravada Buddhism Doctrine of the Elders, the branch of Buddhism that spread across southeast Asia

Tie-beam The horizontal beam connected to the feet of the rafters to prevent them spreading under the weight of the roof

Traiphum Three worlds of Buddhist cosmology

Traidhatuka The threefold world

Tympanum Space between a lintel and the arch above it

Vientiane City of the Moon, present capital of Laos

Urna The mark between the Buddha's eyebrows,

Ushnisha Protuberance at the top of the Buddha's head

Vara Giving benediction

Vishnu Hindu god of preservation and compassion

Vinaya Rules and regulations of monastic life

Vitarka Gesture of preaching

Wat Lao or Thai Buddhist temple

Yantra Symbolic diagram

Yoni Female generative organ, and thus the origin of life.

INDEX